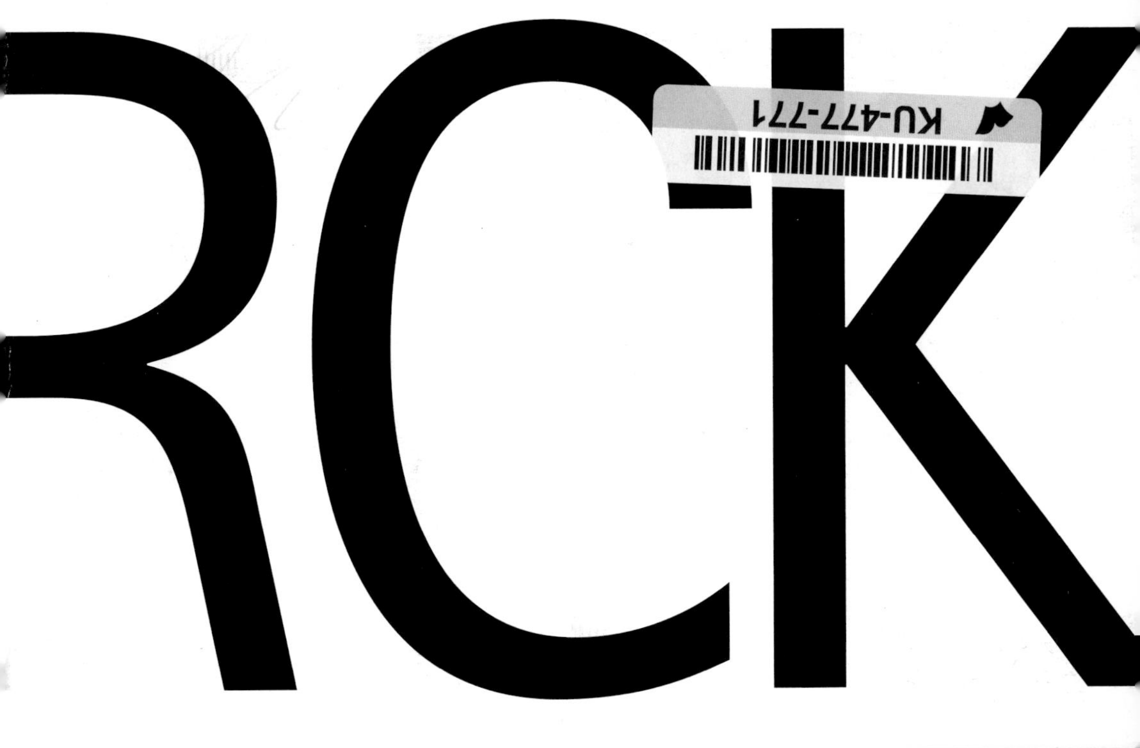
RCK

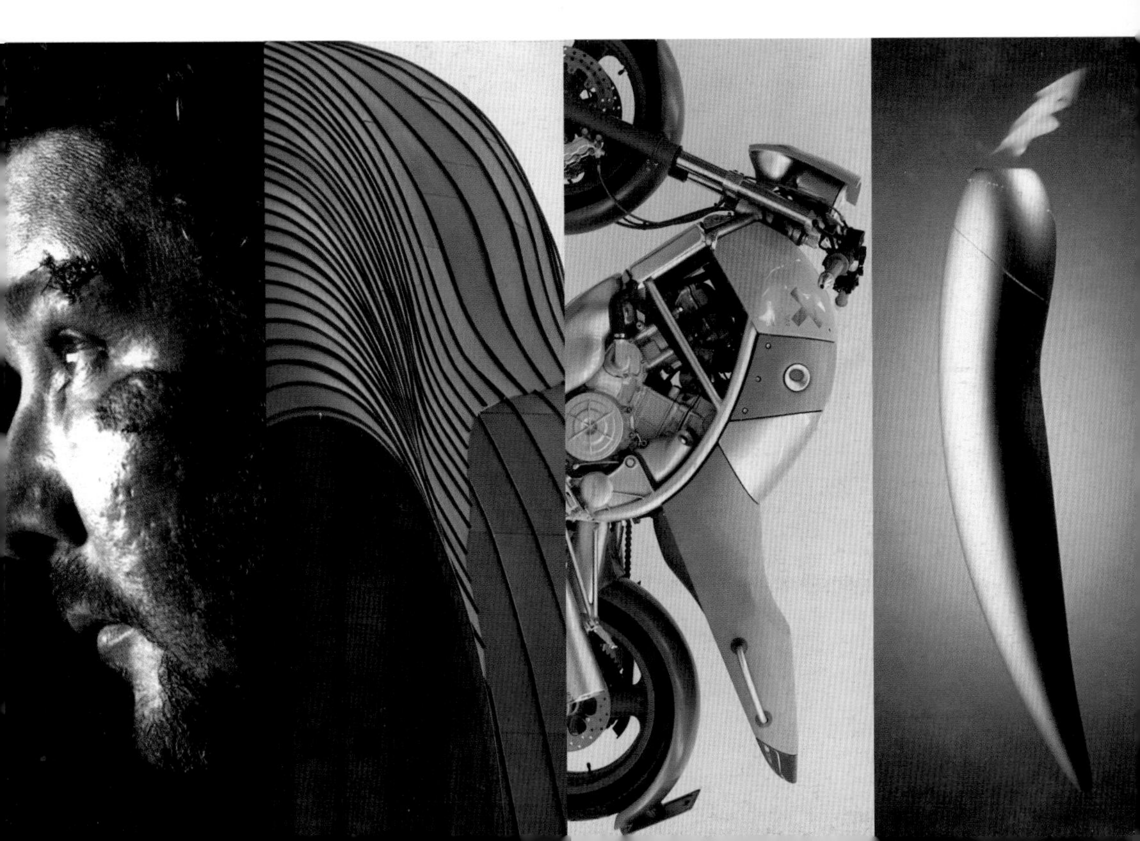

This book is for Armelle, with love.

I have a special debt to Laurence King, who invited me to work with Starck on the *International Design Yearbook* four years ago. If meeting Starck then was exciting, our subsequent encounters and our work together on this book have been exhilarating. Starck's enthusiasm, humor, and sense of perfection have been an inspiration.

My thanks also to the members of Starck's "tribe" who have helped with this book, especially Bruno Borrione, Benedicte Deverre, Pierre Doze, Cristina Fredi, Thierry Gaugain, Patrik Granquist, Anne Marie Grué, Vesta Mauch-Lassalle, and Sonia Ortiz Alcun. Others who have offered help and advice include Paul Acker, Albrecht Bangert, Iain Boal, Chris Foges, Martin Pawley, Otto Riewoldt, Joy Roffey, and Giuliano Zampi.

For their welcome in Paris, thanks to Patricia and Jean-Marie, and Paule, Jean-Louis, and Antoine.

Keith Lovegrove has my special thanks for his careful and inventive work on the graphic design, as does Elizabeth Johnson for her editorial vigilance.

To quote Starck, "à l'amour, nuit et jour, toujours l'amour."

Conway Lloyd Morgan, London 1998

First published in the United States of America
by UNIVERSE PUBLISHING
A Division of Rizzoli International Publications, Inc.
300 Park Avenue South
New York, NY 10010

00 01 02 / 10 9 8 7 6 5 4 3 2

Printed in Italy

Library of Congress Cataloging-in-Publication Data
Morgan, Conway Lloyd.
Philippe Starck / Conway Lloyd Morgan.
p. cm.
ISBN 0-7893-0227-6
1. Starck, Philippe, 1949- —Criticism and interpretation.
2. Design—France—History—20th century. I. Starck, Philippe, 1949- . II. Title.
NK1449.Z9S7236 1999
745.2'092—dc21 98-48499

Contents

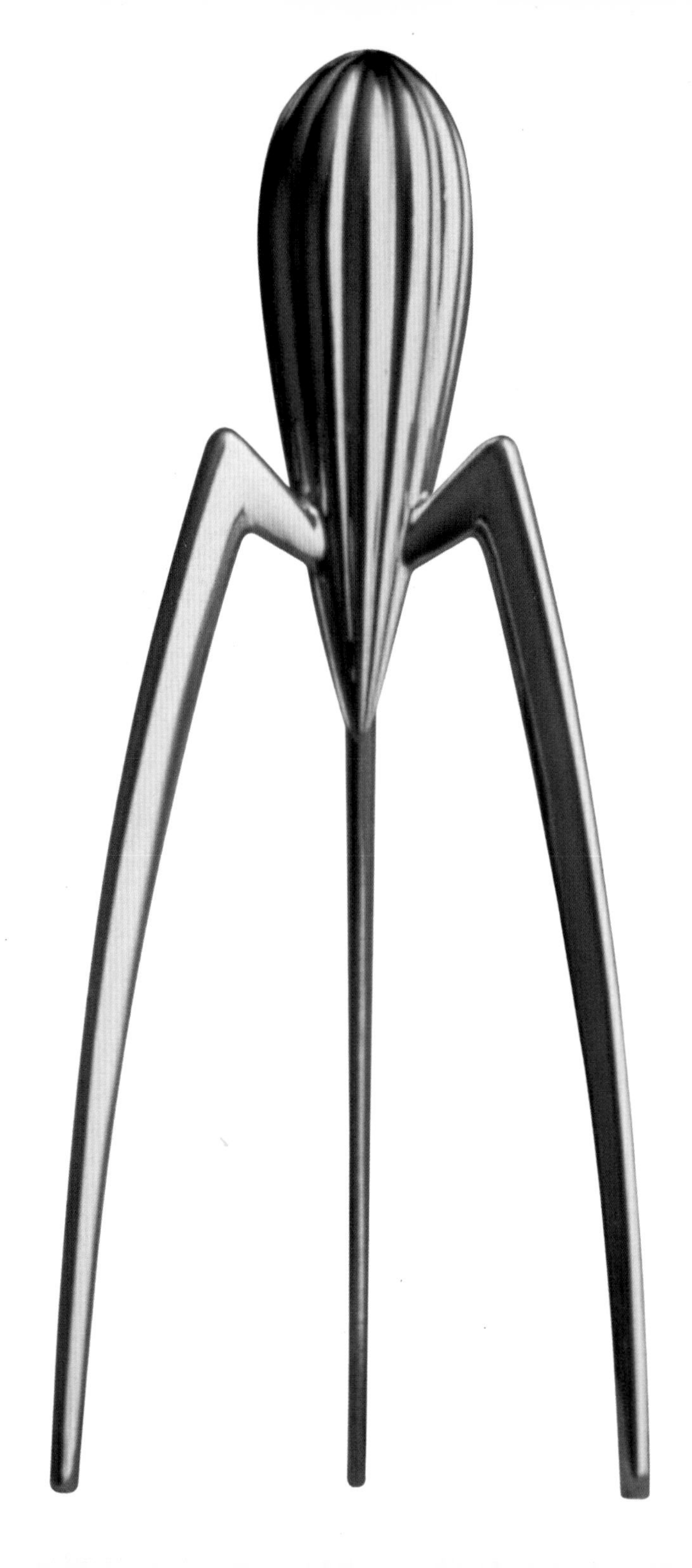

This is not a very good lemon squeezer: but that's not its only function. I had this idea that when a couple gets married it's the sort of thing they would get as a wedding present. So when the new husband's parents come round, he and his father sit in the living room with a beer, watching television, and the new mother-in-law and daughter-in-law sit in the kitchen to get to know each other better. "Look what we got as a present," the daughter-in-law will say. . . .

I created this toothbrush because it's a basic nonproduct. Everyone needs one, and they're all much the same. But I thought that if, first thing in the morning, you had something bright and cheerful sitting on the shelf waiting for you, it would be like opening the bathroom window onto a summer landscape every day.

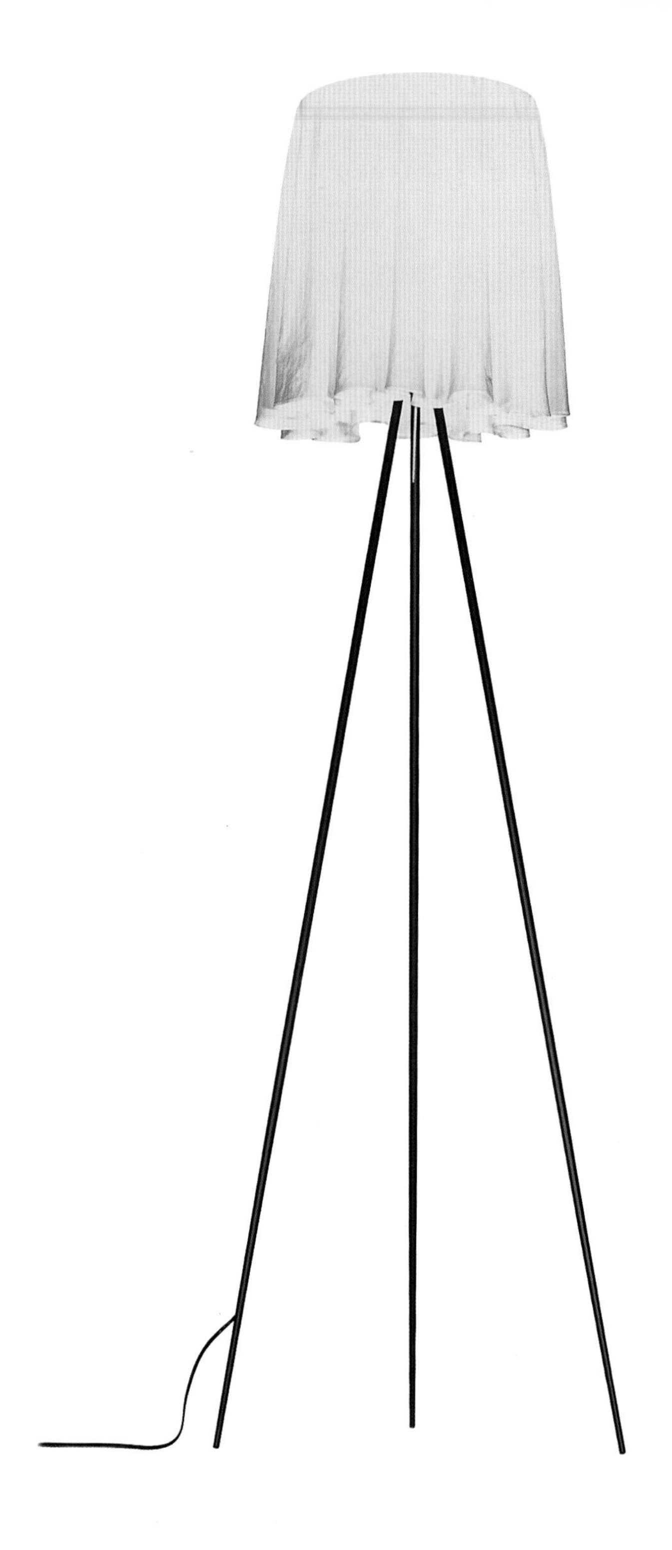

What is needed are people who have already achieved something, who can be a bit more objective, who are not motivated by hunger, people who are capable of saying no.

The Rosy Angelis lamp was designed to commemorate the 1966 standard lamp by Achille Castiglioni, "who invented the everyday with a bit of string."

A few years ago I suggested the concept of "nondesign": the designer would disappear behind a sort of collective memory. The Miss Sissi lamp is an example. You can't say I designed it; everybody did. When it first appeared it seemed totally reactionary, but a moment later it became the new reference point. It has undoubtedly been the most copied and imitated lamp in the world.

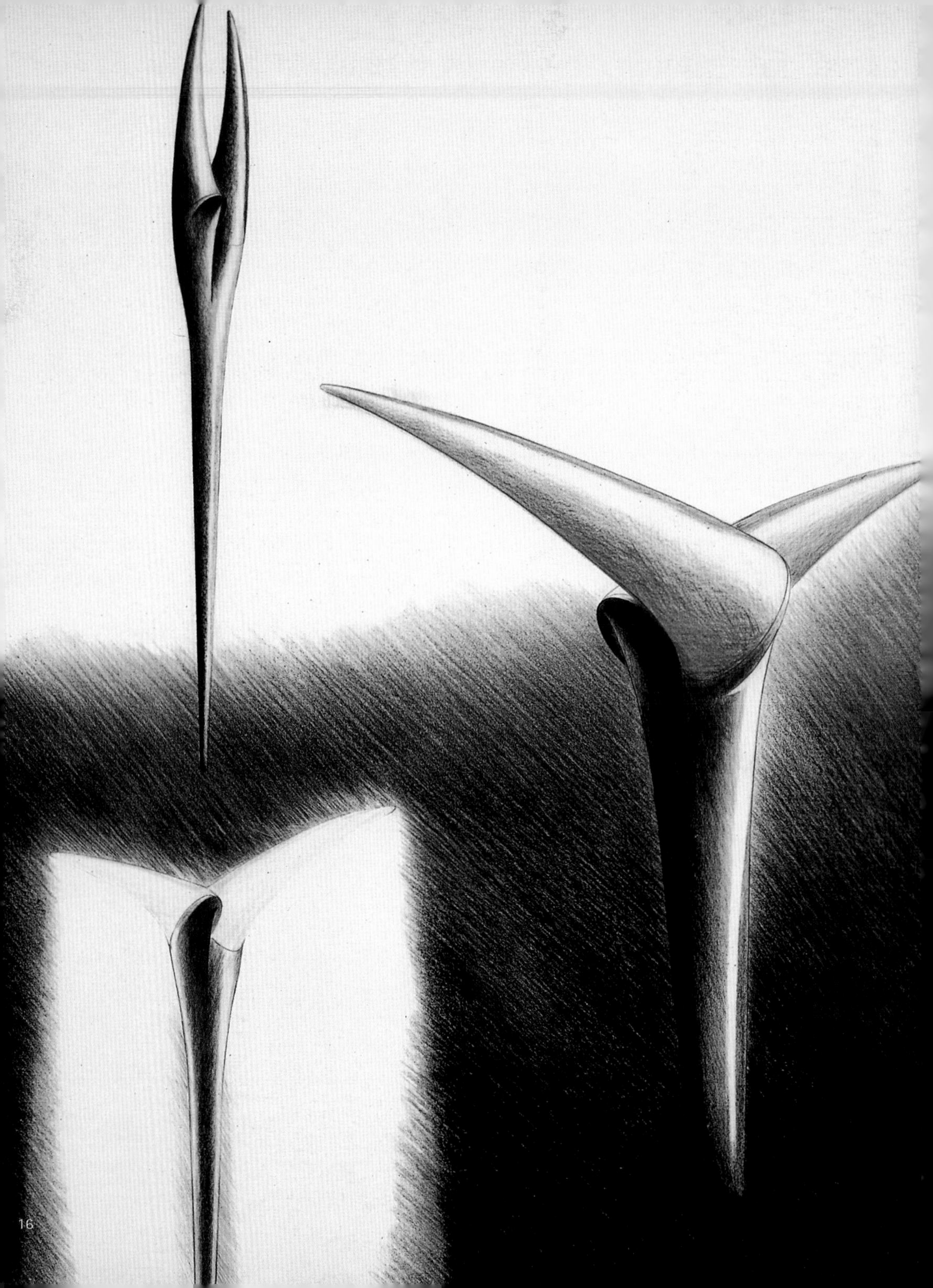

I am all for economy, in the psychoanalytical sense of the term, the economy of everything. A product that achieves its obligations with a minimum of means. I like to touch things at the root, at the point where no more division is possible. The simpler an object is, the harder it is to make it: decoration always conceals something else.

These sunglasses and spectacles are not design, just pure technology. Alain Mikli and I worked on a joint for the side pieces that would be completely articulable. Supple movement in all directions. We found the model in the human clavicle and translated it into engineering terms. It is a question of finding a new relationship between people and materials: a biodesign.

In no case do I create for the sake of creating: I don't have the imagination for that, it doesn't interest me. I prefer to take the everyday things we all have to do, like washing or keeping out of the rain, and give these simple necessities a fifth dimension, a depth that gives an ordinary, necessary object the opportunity to speak of other things. It's part of a simple proposition, to make people happier by making their everyday lives better. And so give back sense and interest to urban living.

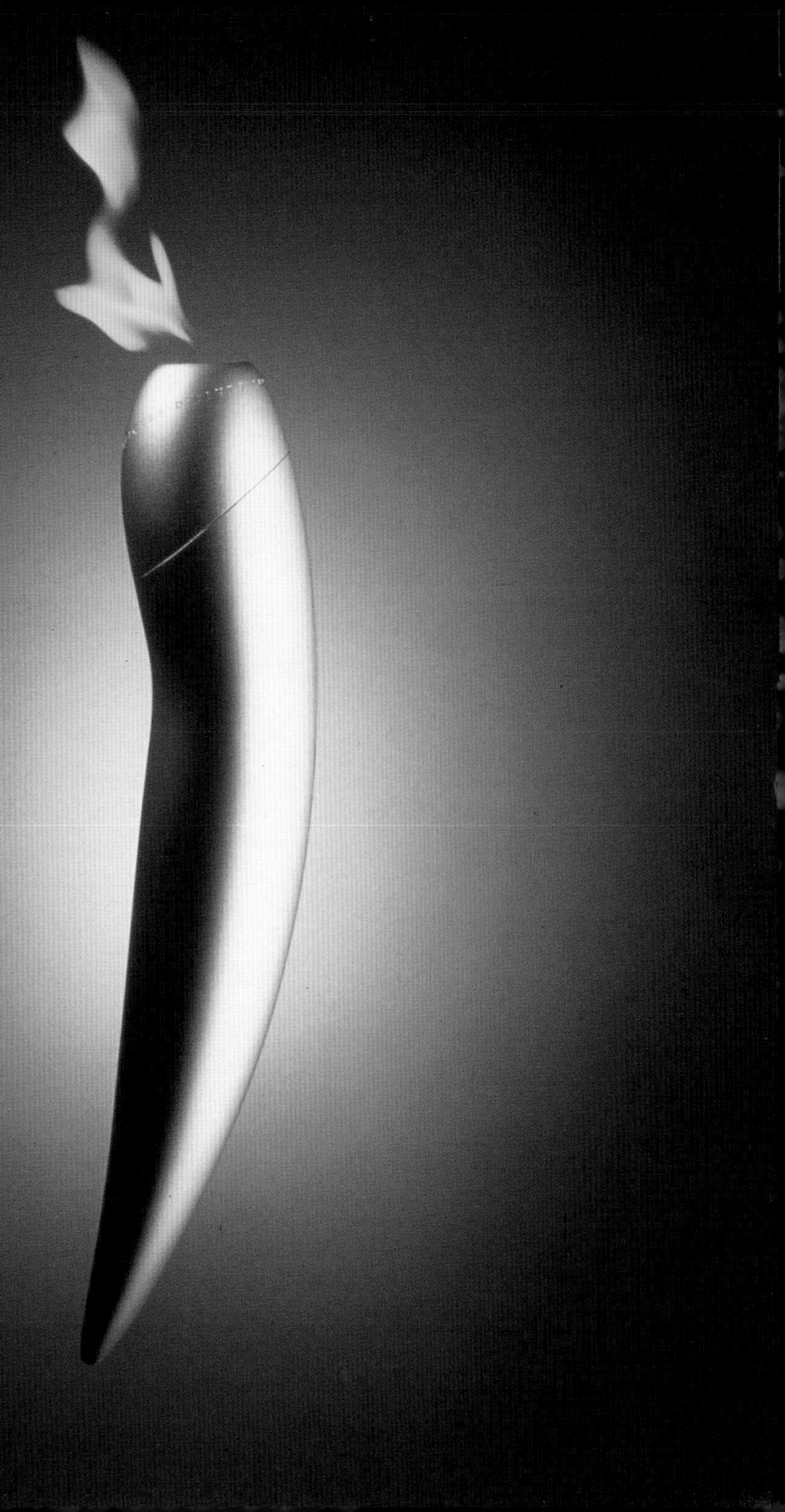

I hope there is no such thing as a "Starck style." What I do see in my own work, and that only when I see an exhibition of it, is a certain logic of thought and work, and a mode of action that is clearly more political than "designer." It is a way of doing things, a point of view, and a kind of violence in action. It's a style of not having a style.

ORGANIC
THAI RICE
OAO

Food has always interested me a lot—because it is everyday, very human, and also curiously taboo. A key idea for me is that today we are at a pivotal point. "Grand" foods, because of their symbolic value, are becoming democratized, which is positive, but also banal, which is negative. We must be ready to welcome unhesitatingly new foods, which owe nothing to the past or a false image of tradition, but which can be absolutely appropriate for new modes of living and eating. We must accept with no reservations the idea that food, like society, is in mutation all the time.

Engineering, and French engineering especially, is something I have always found very beautiful. French engineering is, above all, poetic, compared to American, German, or Japanese engineering, which is purely functional. French engineering (and Italian engineering, too, in a way), is not about producing the most efficient or most commercial solution, but about producing the most elegant intellectual form. French engineering is a mental exercise based on the twin obligations of innovation and elegance, which is why it is the most beautiful in the world. And I always had the intuition that that was the state to be in—one of poetry linked to the real world. What interests me today is deciphering the poetry of the everyday.

André Starck leaned to fly before World War II in a Mignet Pou, and was a pioneer light-aircraft manufacturer in the reconstruction of the French aviation industry after the war. He designed, built, and flew several monoplane and biplane designs for club aircraft and trainers.

The magician stands on the spotlit stage. The assistant, with sequins glinting in the glare, stands nearby. A bashful member of the audience allows billiard balls to pass in one ear and out the other and cards to fall from sleeves. The audience applauds, but knows there is a trick in the trick. While they admire the mastery and the skill, they remember that "the swiftness of the hand deceives the eye." It is all showmanship and no substance.

There are some who see the work of French designer Philippe Starck in similar terms. They see, and sometimes even disparage, his effortless visual fluency, his ability to move from one area to another, his incessant production, his endless novelty. But they admire his skill. In the early part of his career he was regularly referred to as an "*enfant terrible*": he was an idiot savant who could conjure design seemingly out of thin air. His own public personality did little to discourage this view, and remarks such as "The rest of the French design business lives on the work I've turned down" did little to endear Starck to his contemporaries. Nor did his lifestyle; instead of being seen at all the best openings and events, he remained resolutely private, in fact too busy enjoying his work to have time to socialize. Public perception of him is reflected in newspaper headlines of the times. "The Fabulous Style of the Man with No Taste" was one; "French Design's Bad Boy Makes Good" was another.

Behind Starck's work and his approach to it lies a simple and subtle, complex and compelling concept, formed from his analysis of humanity and society, and from a clear perception of what he feels is an urgent problem that faces not merely design but all of us. This concept can be stated in a single word, "love." The prudery of much of Western society forbids us to see love as a real and potent idea. "Love" is easily misinterpreted because we use it so broadly. We use it to refer to passion, whether Christian or sexual, to altrusim and charity, and to pride and patriotism. For Starck, "love is what defines us as human, as a society, as a civilization: without it we will cease to be human, arbitrary as a mental construct the idea of love may be."

"Christopher Columbus did not discover America, because he did not name it, or know in fact what he had found. Things exist only if you give them names and recognize them. What we must recognize about being human is that it is a poetic concept whose principal defining factor is love: love in the sense of maternal love, which in turn originates from a shared desire to protect and nurture the species." Starck's proposition is neither scientific nor philosophical dogma; rather it is a basis for action. He is an autodidact, but he endorses the scientific method of proceeding by thorough and impartial analysis. "I'm a functionalist, not a poet," he remarks.

"The other key aspect of humankind," Starck continues, "is that as a species, as a society, as a civilization, we are endlessly and continuously in a state of **mutation.** We have to accept that, so we cannot stand still and hope change will stop. It is impossible for change to stop. The main change in the last twenty centuries of human history has been humankind's power over matter, and the relentless search for material goods. With the extension of mechanization at the beginning of the twentieth century this race for material power has been faster and even faster, and always at the expense of love." Now, at the end of the twentieth century, Starck feels that the danger is not only that love is sacrified for materialism, but that the very concept of love itself risks being abandoned. The history of cruelty, war, famine, and political indifference to human suffering of just the last decade—supposedly the one that saw the cold war end and peace begin—suggests that material comfort does not create caring societies. Starck has spoken out often against the rise of **neofascism** in France and throughout the world, and against the failure of European governments to intervene in Bosnia.

"If the very idea of love is forgotten by humankind," Starck points out, "we are not merely losing a mental concept. We are losing our unique distinction from brute beasts, and so we will lose the family, society, and civilization along

Hot Bertaa, 1990

with it. It is a structural problem, like fishes forgetting how to breathe underwater. Suppose one day we realized that panthers were becoming obese, or giraffes suddenly had short necks; we would realize that there was a profound problem with those species. But we do not realize that the human race is also an endangered species because of the progressive loss of love."

The rise of materialism has created both greed, which kills love, and, in a more sinister fashion, passivity. This passivity is shown by the feeling people have that control over their future has passed from their hands, and even from the politicians' hands. "There is," according to Starck, "the idea that the networks of power and influence are now controlled by large multinational companies, and those networks are too strong to break. So people give up, they resign their hope, and this resignation has almost become part of the social structure. Yes, there are small revolutions from time to time, driven by desperate need for food or shelter, but in the developed societies of the world, revolution is not even thought of as a possibility. "What good would it serve?" people say. "They—the multinationals—have all the power." Yes, you can oppose a government, but how do you oppose people who are living off you, who are permanently seeking, through market research, through publicity, through the media, to deliver what they think you

desire? They are behind the one-way mirror, watching everything, the better to supply satisfaction. Opposing that is a very difficult task; it's almost like fighting yourself. Because satisfaction is, by and large, desirable, except that it is only material satisfaction, which is not enough. I am not against commerce, but against consumption as the only purpose of society."

What, then, is the solution to this problem of resignation and the dominance of materialism? Starck proposes two related strategies. The first he terms "a new civics": it is based on the necessity of individual participation in a consensual society. In the introduction to the 1997 *International Design Yearbook* he claimed, "We must invent a new morality. Today, too many societies are tipping too easily into antisocial forms. Under respectable pretexts of liberty, some social movements are advocating antisocial actions which will ineluctably lead to repression and to a partial or total loss of individual liberty. This tide must be changed, by inventing new codes of social life that will redefine the extent of both our individual liberty and our social duty. The reinvention of morality is a return to a modern civics. Without such individual decisions of conscience, there is no way forward for today's society. It is out of the question to imagine that a modern society, in which so many have a participatory role, can survive in a state of anarchy. A

humane, intelligent, responsible social order, in which generosity and mutual respect are the rule, are the only path to freedom."

The second strategy is against **consumption** not through denial, which is reactionary and unrealistic, but through what he terms "the immaterial object." "We should take Raymond Loewy's slogan `La laideur se vend mal' ['The ugly doesn't sell well,' the French title for Loewy's 1952 book *Never Leave Well Enough Alone*] and turn it around: `Make ugly products so they don't sell!' But Loewy's slogan, and the attitude of designers at the time, dictated the design process for decades. It was about making products that would sell; it was wholly and relentlessly commercial. That idea is now obsolete. A system based on consumption, as we have seen and are seeing, has the seeds of its own collapse endemic within it. It is, in itself, an untenable system. But we now have the **technology** to create the immaterial object, the nonobject. The twenty-first century will be the century of the immaterial: there will be no need to possess to enjoy. If we can push back materialism, there will be room for love to evolve. So the next century will be both immaterial and human: humanity will achieve progress by understanding that what was material can become immaterial—in both senses of each word—in favor of a direct, human contact with the world and others."

In this vision of the future, designers have a special responsibility as actors in this process: they have a duty to facilitate the evolution of love, because love is both a human quality and an abstract concept, and it can be made to evolve, and be fostered, through human agency. As Starck wrote in the *International Design Yearbook*, "The old idea of the designer as a mediator is also wholly wrong. A designer as mediator is inevitably involved in the process of production. The designer should be a doctor, listening to the patient, seeking out the best cure for the condition. In some cases where the illness is serious, a medicine of intense sophistication is required; in some a traditional remedy suffices; in others good advice is all that is needed. So the designer of tomorrow has a much wider role in and toward society, and design's means of expression are not limited to production systems. Production is only one means of expression, and it should be the last resort. All the other possible solutions, not involving material consumption should be explored first. And if production is necessary, that production should be ethical. For example, reorganizing a bus timetable to reduce city center pollution is design–it is honest work that serves social ends. It is a 'design production' even though no consumption of material is involved. It is pure design."

Starck approaches this desperate situation, with optimism and even glee, because he now sees that the evolution of

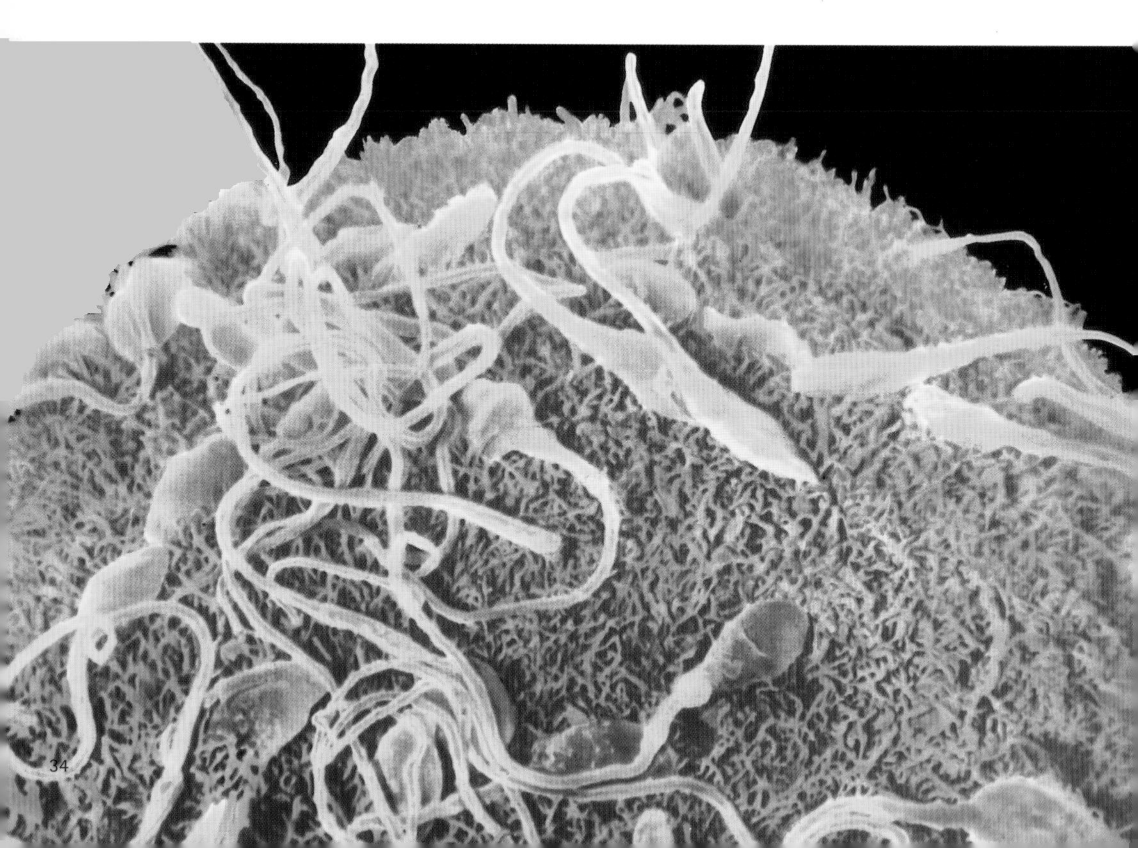

technology—through computing and communication, through biology and genetics, through physics and nano-science—is, almost at the last moment, becoming able to deliver the right solutions. Surprisingly, this current optimism is a complete change from the morbidity that colored his view some years ago, when the problems he now sees as so pressing were equally apparent, but the possibility of resolving them less so. It still takes considerable moral courage for a designer to assume such an exposed position, not merely in speaking out about society's problems but in creating an active program of projects to address them. But Starck's view is that designers, as agents of change in society, have not merely a passive obligation to do good, but also a positive one.

The purpose of this book is to explore how Starck's approach to society and design translates into his current work. We will also try to assess the validity of his thinking as a general principle of design for the twenty-first century. But before doing that we need to look at how Starck has developed his current design philosophy over time, and how he has achieved his present reputation and success. The image of Starck as the clever design magician or as the successful *enfant terrible* is itself a public illusion—he has always been a most serious, concerned, and involved designer.

At the 1996 Paris Furniture Show, Philippe Starck gave a lecture. The room was packed, but I found a seat next to a student who was wearing the double headphones provided for the simultaneous translation and holding open a large notebook, pen poised. Starck began speaking, without notes but using slides, and the student bent over the pad and began writing furiously. At one point Starck described the commission for the Olympic torch for the 1992 Olympic Games at Albertville. "What is the essence of the Olympic flame?" he asked rhetorically. "It burns and it runs. So, take one fireproofed athlete's arm, immerse in fuel, apply match, and run like blazes!" He explained this with leaps and bounds, miming the worried look on the athlete's face, while we roared with laughter. The student did not hear the laughter through the headphones and carried on making notes. Laughing at Starck's antics with the rest, I smiled to myself about the gullibility of students.

But thinking about it later I realized that the laugh was on me, not on the student. The point Starck was making was that the Olympic symbolism resides in the flame, not the torch; so long as you can have the flame, you do not need a torch at all. It is an approach to design that begins by asking, "What is the necessary minimum?" (which can be nothing), not "What do I do?" Between his visually dazzling work and his profoundly serious message sits the public persona of

Starck himself, ambiguous and gleeful, bumptious and self-deprecating, complex and paradoxical. How did this person, and this persona, come to have such an influential role in contemporary design?

Starck was born in January 1949 in Neuilly, a prosperous bourgeois suburb on the northern side of Paris. His father was an aircraft engineer at a time when the concept of engineering was broader and wider than it is today. His grandparents were Russian Jews. Starck was not a brilliant pupil at school (the painter Gérard Garouste, who was at school with him, recalls that he was "into all sorts of mad projects and extraterrestrial ideas"), and Starck always claims that "design found me, not me design."

He continues, "My mother and I lived alone, rather isolated. We didn't know what I should do in life—become a chef, perhaps. At the age of fifteen I was rather feminine—feminine, not effeminate—and my mother's lover, a Catharist priest, said one day, 'He's bound to become homosexual, so he'd better be a designer.' He gave me the name of a design school and I went there—I always did what I was told. When I arrived, there were drawings hanging on the walls, all of them on tracing paper, A4 size, drawn in soft lead pencil. I still always draw that way." Starck joined the Ecole Nissim de Camondo in Paris in the mid-1960s, but it seems he already had a talent for drawing, and this led him to the school.

He has also recalled, in the competition for the Bordeaux Airport Control Tower project, "My childhood bed was under my father's drawing board, and I had to move his compasses, templates, and slide rules in order to go to sleep, as if I was born in the air. The wallpaper seemed to be all tailfins and **curving arches,** elegantly and competently drawn. I grew up on airfields. . . . My father was a humble participant, happy and unhappy, in the great and continuing adventure of French aviation, and I owe everything to the spirit and genius of French engineering." His father also had a sense of humor. Starck tells of visiting a science museum with his father and seeing a machine gun: "My father said, 'It's a gun which fires twenty rounds a second—it's what killed Napoleon.' Later, at school, when the teacher asked about Napoleon's death, Starck promptly shared his new knowledge with the class, to the teacher's annoyance. His father had meant that quick-firing weapons had destroyed Napoleonic infantry and cavalry tactics fifty years after Napoleon's death. The incident taught Starck something about ambiguity, and left him with a certain distrust of formal education. Not that he had much of a formal education: his parents separated when he was eleven, and he spent the next few years playing truant, riding around the Parc de Saint Cloud on a small motorbike, fighting with local gangs. When he did return to school it was mainly to sit at the back of the class and draw. The drawings were, he once said, mainly of

Dole Melipone, 1981

sophisticated torture chambers for his teachers, complete with containers to gather and recycle the blood! "The teachers were very kind to me," he recalled, "though some used to confiscate my drawings—I think because they liked them themselves!" After leaving school—he cannot remember, he says, at what date and with what qualification—he lived alone at home, hardly going out, drawing and looking at magazines. "I lived in a room that was not so large, with a drawing board, no bed, and a meter-high pile of magazines, in a state of near-schizophrenia," he later said in a magazine interview.

Formal design school did not teach him much—apart from the use of tracing paper. In the early 1970s he set up his first business, making inflatables and kit furniture, and worked as an artistic director for Pierre Cardin. He also began designing night clubs: La Main Bleue (Blue Hand) in 1976 and Les Bains Douches (Baths and Showers) in 1978, amid a stream of others, including La Main Jaune and Le Chalet du Lac. He also worked as a store interior designer and created trade-fair stands for clients such as Kansai, Yamamoto, and Creeks. Little evidence of these ephemeral productions remains, but some idea of their exuberance can be gleaned from later projects, such as La Cigale concert hall in Paris, the Theatriz restaurant in Mexico, or the Manin in Tokyo, and stores such as the Hugo Boss shop in Paris. The early clubs'

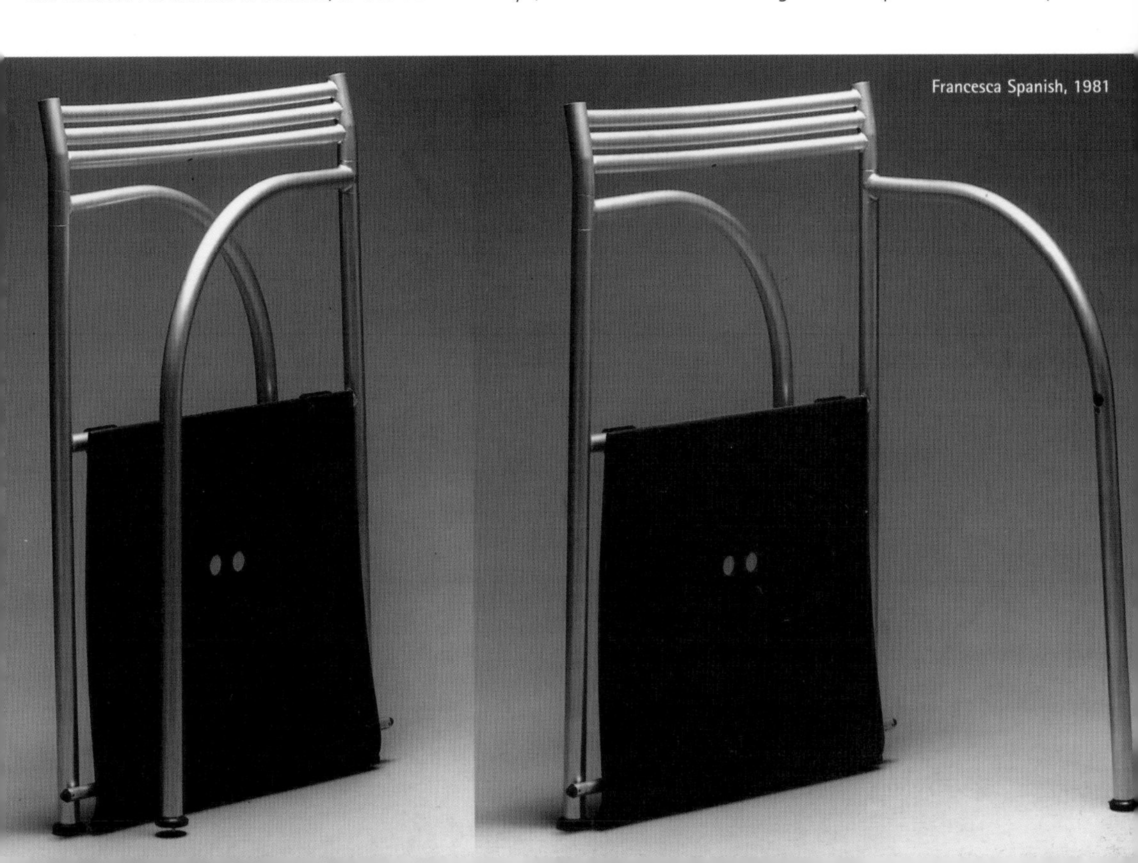
Francesca Spanish, 1981

vigorous personalities, and the personality of their creator, had a strong impact at the time: Starck's clubs were the place to be seen. One magazine featured an interview with Starck at La Main Bleue in which the interviewer was a fellow clubber, fashion designer Jean-Paul Gaultier. When Les Bains Douches was redesigned by Starck in 1981, even the serious left-wing newspaper *Libération* sent its correspondent to take a look at social realism meeting punk on the dance floor. Starck had hung the space with enormous red flags and covered the floors in synthetic snow. The menu was printed in Cyrillic lettering, and on the walls were Soviet film posters and a portrait of a dog (an allusion to the mongrel shown in portraits of Stalin in his "father of the people at home" pose).

Starck explained to *Libération* that the Stalino-Trotskyist décor "was more a caprice than anything else. I love red flags and red velvet. While I hate fascism, I adore fascist architecture, and my first idea was to make the setting even more 'supreme Soviet' than it is—but that might have been disturbing. So I've just thrown in a few hints and suggestions. The design is mainly a kind of game with materials, particularly mahogany and velvet. In my interiors, I think I do achieve an emotional contact with the people who use the space." *Libération* found the place "sympathetic and original," though perhaps more Marx Brothers than Karl. The Russian ambassador to France never did come, despite an open invitation.

Les Bains Douches, 1981

What Starck seems to have captured in his design work is the nihilist frenzy of the time: economic prosperity under right-wing governments in an enduring cold war led to a certain indifferent decadence. Philip K. Dick portrayed such fractured societies in his stories and books, which Starck read avidly at the time, and in which he found the names for many early designs. A similar theme emerged in his work at Café Costes two or three years later, but by then France's government had changed, with the left at last coming to power under President Mitterrand. The new president invited a group of young French designers, including Starck, to redecorate the presidential apartments at the Elysée Palace. Starck's success at the Elysée and at Costes established his international reputation as an interior designer and architect, particularly in his collaborations with the hotel entrepreneur Ian Schrager, and in his work in Japan. His success in this field is due in part to his ability to build references to the ambiguities and uncertainties of everyday life in settings that are wholly original, as at Les Bains Douches or later in the Moondog project. Two factors contribute to this. The first is an endless interest in and fascination with the world around him, in all its forms. "I started design school as an autodidact, and so kept an open eye on the problems I was given there. And my polymorphic curiosity means I'm as much interested in new technologies as I am in painting and sculpture, theater and cinema, which isn't the case for all

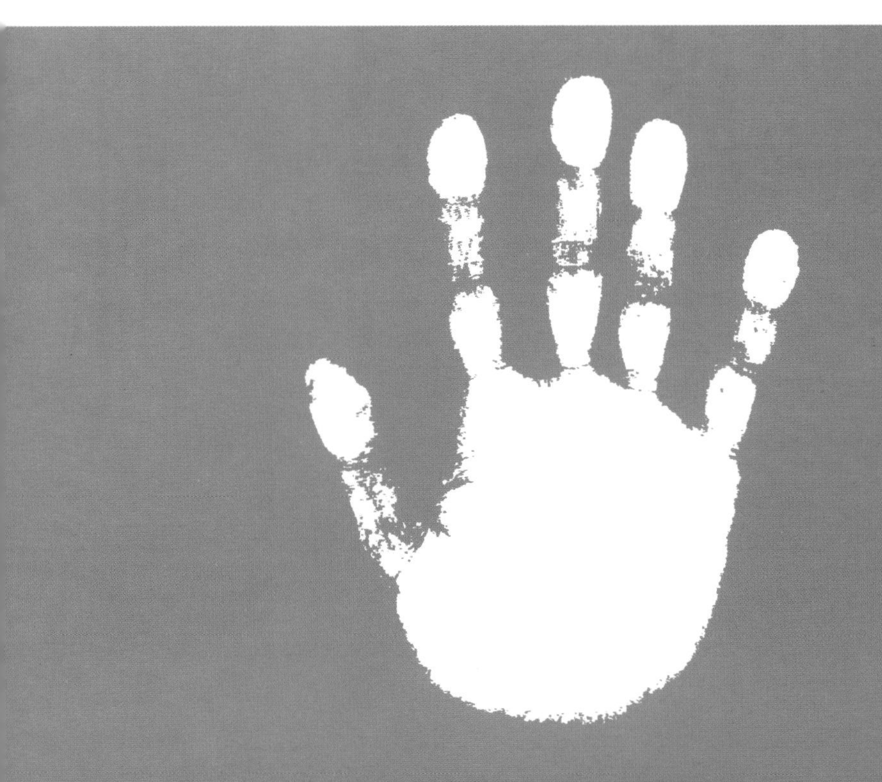

my contemporaries," he said in a 1985 interview. The second quality is his uncompromising honesty of purpose–his ability to overlay a scientific approach with a child's wonder and an artist's **eye for form.** This is the consequence, perhaps, of innate gifts shaped by the disciplined engineering background of his father and his own random education. Starck arrived on the design stage at a particularly appropriate time, as Cristina Morosi pointed out in a 1985 article in *Modo*: "So who is this Starck the French call the 'enfant terrible' of design? A natural talent, a loner who castigates trends and acknowledges no debt to the great Italian design masters, whom he regards as tired clichés? Or, one of those clever stunts the American star system excels at, and France's design landscape (lacking venerable, old trees to cherish and vigorous young shrubs to cultivate) so badly needs at the moment? Probably both. Certainly, his design approach, his engineer's rather than artist's discipline, as he likes to call it, his ability to be 'fashionable' despite his affirmations that he doesn't particularly like it when he is, all have their interest.

"More than anything else, Philippe Starck represents that new breed of professionals who have successfully transferred the mechanics of style to design, who invest more in their own images than in products, who try to meet people's expectations rather than find outlets for personal creativity and self-expression. . . . His secret is to have understood

La Cigale, 1981

that something has run its course in the designer-manufacturer relationship, that the respective crafts have to be reinvented, that people want symbolic products they can use as emblems of tribal recognition."

Morosi's analysis of the convergence of design and fashion was prescient: this convergence can be seen in the new range of 1990s magazines that treat design, fashion, sexual behavior, and food as aspects of "lifestyle," and in the evolution of traditional fashion magazines into new roles and forms. She is inaccurate, though, in berating Starck for not acknowledging the Italian design tradition: he himself pays homage to Achille Castiglioni, Alessandro Mendini, Denis Santachiara, and Alberto Meda, among others, on the endpapers of his 1996 book, *Starck*, and he sometimes describes himself as "an Italian designer who happens to be French." While he understands the important role of the media, and the necessity for a successful designer working across a range of areas to have a strong public image, there is a radical difference between Starck's societally based approach to design and the style-led world of fashion. Starck's intuition was not simply that the old order had changed, but went further: with the ending of the old order the opportunities for the designer had changed, and the obligations on the designer, toward society, self, and technology, needed to be redefined.

Boutique Hugo Boss, 1991

The Le Moult house, built on a site on the Ile St. Germain on the outskirts of Paris, was commissioned in 1985 as a private house by Bruno Le Moult and his wife, friends of Starck. The site (which now adjoins Starck's own main office) was long and narrow, running down to a branch of the Seine. On this 21-by-210-foot site Starck built what he has called "a sphinx."

The house is on two levels at the street side, which spread into three floors and a roof terrace toward the river, following the contours of the terrain. Seen from the street, a double-height window is framed by two narrow staircase ramps rising to the first-floor level. It looks rather like a piece of furniture, a tallboy, in which the family treasures are exhibited behind glass. But the original intention, as the writer Franco Bertoni has pointed out, was for the stairways to rise and then drop down to the entrances, in the manner of the tomb passages in Egyptian pyramids. The site was too small for this, and so the final solution should perhaps be termed a ziggurat rather than a sphinx, especially given the pattern of internal staircases and stepped ramps that give access to the different interior levels. The ramps follow a curved line, which is echoed in the internal walls on the upper main floor, just as the internal staircases are canted to widen as they rise. Like a sphinx, the house sits on its site with its paws set out in front.

Le Moult

The Le Moult house is particularly exciting for the degree of subtlety and complexity packed into such a small and unpromising site. The interior spaces, fitted out with Starck's own furniture, are elegant, while the whole has a dominant sense of depth and mystery. It is an apt echo of the morbidity and élan that characterized, in equal measure, Starck's other design work at the time. As Francesco Bertoni notes, this same ability to create interior surprise within an almost forbidding exterior can also be found in Starck's 1992 proposal for a cubic housing block in Venice, California.

The Le Moult house also provided a key element in another project that was never achieved, the "rue Starck" at Issy-les-Moulineaux, a proposed development of the rue Pierre Poli, where his offices and the Le Moult house stand. The Le Moult house was to be flanked by a miniature Nani Nani building, a version of the Venice project, and the Angle project for Antwerp from 1991, a building set into the ground at an angle but restored to verticality by its window bars which are at an angle to the walls, as well as a number of other buildings. These totems to a future definition of the city, in which the external appearance is not symbolically related to the life within, remain Starck's only proposal for a large-scale urban project to date.

The Café Costes design brief called for "somewhere as beautiful and sad as the railway station buffet in Prague"; this was in 1982, when the memory of the Prague Spring was not recent, but the image of a city with a proud history was a potent one for Parisians, for whom the promises of 1968 seemed also to have failed.

One place where they had failed was the Halles quarter of Paris, originally the central food market of the city. Part of the area's redevelopment yielded the Pompidou Center by Piano and Rogers, one of the most popular contemporary buildings in France. But the commercial redevelopment of the adjacent main Halles site, despite a number of bold proposals, was banal—rows of shops set on the slopes of an excavated bowl. (Parisians called it "le trou des Halles," a pun on the term for the orifice for suppositories.)

Café Costes became the in place in Les Halles. The café, which closed in 1987, had an outdoor pavement area, a small ground floor on either side of the stairwell, and a large, square room on the lower level lit by a long skylight. There the three-legged Costes chairs, designed by Starck, were set against small round tables, while the space was dominated by enormous but redundant pillars. Two of these flanked the narrowing staircase, itself surmounted by a strange eight-numbered clock. The staircase was finished in green, with pale browns and yellows for walls and ceilings. There was

Costes

an immediate ambiguity in these forms: the pillars seemed large enough to support an office block but led to a skylight, which on closer inspection turned out to be artificially backlit. The structures were grandiose but the finishes completely mundane. If this was Prague station, it had a parallel in Vera Chytilova's 1966 underground film *Daisies*, a surreal "rite of passage" tale of two girls who pick up strangers in the station restaurant there.

Starck claims that the three-legged Costes chair was intended to prevent injuries to waiters by reducing by twenty-five percent the number of chair legs they might trip over. It's a delightful conceit, but Parisian waiters are generally quite capable of looking after themselves. Rather, a three-legged chair creates a momentary unease in the user: Will it stand upright? Just like the clock that tells only eight hours, the chair subverts our immediate expectations, in a slightly morbid way. Just as a railway station is about departure and arrival, a site of passage, so the atmosphere of Café Costes was tinged with uncertainty and doubt. This was partly the influence of the designer's own preoccupations—death and angst were themes he often referred to at the time—but the place derives its appeal from the recognition of such emotions by the patrons. Café Costes was a **subtle, cold mirror** of the lack of purpose and sense of self many felt in the early 1980s, of the shifting meanings and enduring ambiguities of contemporary society.

The election of François Mitterrand as president of the French Republic in the early 1980s marked not only a major change of power from right to left wing, but also a new era for architecture and design. He instigated the series of *grands projets* that during his years in office would see the construction of I.M. Pei's Pyramid and Richelieu Wing at the Louvre, Spreckelsen's Grande Arche at La Defense, and Dominique Perrault's new Bibliothèque Nationale (since named the Bibliothèque François Mitterrand in his memory), as well as numerous other buildings outside Paris. In addition, he invited a group of contemporary interior designers to redecorate the presidential apartment at his official residence, the Elysée Palace in Paris. His minister of culture, Jack Lang, selected the designers, including Starck.

His original commission was for the president's personal office and his bedroom, but for practical reasons the commission for the bedroom was transferred to Jean-Michel Wilmotte, and Starck instead was asked to design the bedroom of the president's wife, Danielle Mitterrand. (Roland Cecil-Sportes designed the main salon; Marc Held, the private drawing room; Annie Tribel, the only woman in the selection, the guest room.)

For Madame Mitterrand's room Starck commissioned a ceiling and dado decoration from his friend the artist Gérard Garouste. The result, a swirling grisaille of surreal forms, was described by Madame Mitterrand as "very playful,

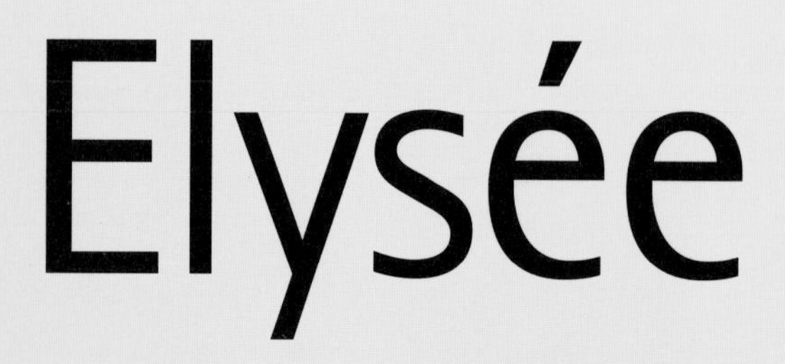

Elysée

luminous, and very reassuring." The bed was framed and hung with curtains, an echo of the great royal beds found in such French châteaux as Chambord and Versailles.

For Mitterrand's own office Starck described his project as having "two parallel levels, distinguished horizontally, representing the subconscious and the conscious, with a fresco by Garouste, a window onto dreams, for the former, and solid grey walls for the latter." Bookcases framed with brushed steel edges and retaining clips were set into the walls. Starck used a first version of the three-legged chair that was to be made famous by the Café Costes the following year, and a glass-topped table with chromed steel frame. (This design was made available commercially some time later.) Starck also introduced the protoype of the Richard III armchair, covered in warm brown leather, resembling from the front a club chair but with the traditional back scooped out to reveal the steel frame. "From the front it's wholly bourgeois, but empty once you turn it round: I like that touch of hypocrisy," Starck said at the time. This ironic comment on the hollow nature of power, as Franco Bertoni has pointed out, was certainly not lost on his "client." Starck's promotion from Parisian nightclubs to the Elysée Palace opened a lot of doors. It was an official confirmation of his status and ability, and orders and commissions from design companies followed.

Japan in the early 1980s was reaping the benefits both of an established social order and of successful economic performance. In motorcycles, cars, and consumer electronics they had evolved from copycat producers to serious market performers, and their financial institutions were beginning to demonstrate their capacity for strategically well placed investment.

Just as in the 1970s Japanese industry had been hungry for Western technology, so Japanese society, particularly the younger urban salarymen, hungered for Western goods and fashions. Urban slang, often a mirror of social aspirations, shows this in a number of Western expressions adopted into Japanese idiom, the process described by Peter Constantine as *wasiego*, in which, for example, the English expression "one pattern" becomes *wunpatan*, meaning boring, or 'drink' becomes *dorinko*.

Not surprisingly, therefore, Japanese companies turned to Western architects and designers, despite the existence of internationally recognized architects in their own country. Starck's reputation as an interior designer à la mode was well known through his furniture design, clubs, and restaurants such as Café Costes. This led to three successive commissions for buildings in Tokyo and Osaka, each different and original, yet having a certain Starck quality.

Japan

The invitation to design the office building that became Nani Nani, completed in 1989, was Starck's first-ever complete architectural commission (he was not technically qualified to be an architect, though he has since been "legitimized" by the French Ordre des Architectes). As he said in a later lecture, "My first question, to myself, was whether I had anything I could legitimately say; if not, the client should go and look for someone else. Even if there was something to say, it was not up to me to try and find a Japanese way of expressing it, nor a Western way. So I thought something fantastical or allegorical might work."

As Starck himself admits, one of the sources for Nani Nani was **Godzilla,** the reawakened dinosaur featured in many Japanese sci-fi films of the 1950s and 1960s. But as he also realized, Godzilla is a phenomenon that can be read on two levels: as a force of lethal darkness, a direct reference to the atomic bomb attacks on Hiroshima and Nagasaki; and as a natural force symbolizing the renaissance of Japan—a threat and a promise. So the Nani Nani building (the name refers to the cry Japanese give when **seeing a ghost,** meaning "What is it? What is it?") is a vast reptilian-green hump, clad in scales. It is a statement of power without sense, yet stable and purposeful—the appropriate monster for the urban sprawl of Tokyo with its unfettered urban planning. But at the same time the interior space is conceived

to deliver the **maximum square footage** per floor, an important consideration in a city where office rents were then the highest in the world.

If the space planning of Nani Nani shows Starck integrating his visual imagination with real estate realities, his Asahi Beer Hall of 1989 shows how architecture and capitalism can interact in other ways. The day after the official opening of the building, the president of Asahi called Starck: "The building appeared on the television news last night on all the major stations," he explained, "and as a result our share values have gone up several points. So the building has paid for itself already!"

Starck's Asahi building is crowned by an enormous orange, bulbous shape ("the largest **Starckerie** in the world," he once called it) that floats above the sloping black hulk of the building. A carrot or a condom, a windsock or a streamer, a frozen cloud or a forgotten dream, it is a form without any figurative content; a truly empty sign that only has emotive context. It is, among other things, immensely fun (unlike the dark support it sits on). It is a counterpoint to the serious exercizing of corporate identities against the Tokyo skyline. It is about enjoyment not power, about relaxation not pressure.

This kind of amorphous curved object is a recurrent visual feature in Starck's work—he coined the term "Starckerie" himself, after all. Sometimes it appears as a menacing, pointed shape, an impossible, broad knife-blade in bright chrome, as at Puzzle in Paris; sometimes as an animal horn, as in the antlerlike supports of the Président M table of 1981, or on the Ara lamp of 1988. On the roof of the 1987 Laguiole factory, it becomes both a blade and a sail. In other materials it become less threatening, most famously on the Mister Meu-Meu stool of 1992, or transforms into something complete, no longer projecting, and so comforting, as with the Alo telephone for Thomson, or the extended curve of the Fluocaril toothbrush.

If there are any artistic parallels for these forms, one is undoubtedly with the work of Constantin Brancusi (Starck acknowledges the debt to Brancusi's *Sleeping Head* in his Moa Moa radio, for example). Brancusi famously declared that, in sculpture, "The forms of naked human beings are no more beautiful than those of toads." His work sought not realism but archetypes. "Beauty is absolute equity," he said. Starck denies any artistic pretensions, yet both he and Brancusi realize that archetypal forms, the portals of collective memory, must be both simple and abstract. As Brancusi also stated, "Simplicity is not an end, but one arrives at simplicity in spite of oneself, in approaching the

real sense of things." For simple, abstract objects to function in awakening unconscious memories, they need tension, for it is tension that tells us that they have purpose, and that necessary tension is best generated through curved forms. Tension can be an expression of balance, of the adjustment of forces into harmony; it can also be an expression of risk, of forces barely contained. Starck's objects and architecture, like Starck's morbid yet optimistic thinking, measure, evince, and control danger and hope in similar ways.

This process can also be seen in Starck's other major architectural project in Japan, the Baron Vert office building in Osaka—the city of merchants, as one Japanese writer described it. Among the drab housing and office blocks lining a six-lane highway, the building appears wholly alien: Does its top, curving to a point, suggest it has been thrust up through the ground, or has it dropped from another dimension? The ferro-concrete frame is covered in green varnished metal panels that flow into curves with the precision of an aircraft's wing and demarcate seven narrow bands of windows, cut into the tension of the surface, as Franco Bertoni has suggested, like a canvas by Lucio Fontana. This tension is still present within the building, where the concrete pushes down over the window frames as if under immense pressure. The Baron Vert was to be at first in red, the Baron Rouge, as it appears in the early

design drawings for the project. But green was felt to be subtler, and perhaps the stronger tone of the red would have distracted the eye from the quiddity of the final construction. It might have led to simpler, more evident metaphors, such as a flame or lantern.

But the Baron Vert is more than an alien object in an alien culture, or an expression of formal mastery. The somber and expressive facade may seem from a distance to be closed and forbidding, but at street level there is a wide, low glazed opening running through the whole depth of the building that gives **a view** onto a Buddhist temple and graveyard behind the building. So what seems like an interposed threat becomes, with a change of perspective, a moment of calm, separating the vigor of the street from the quiet of the cemetery. In the interior, the lowered level and strong horizontality of the windows creates an unusual but comforting space.

The opportunity to work in Japan was an invitation to Starck to explore ideas in a **different culture.** The results show the exploitation of the deliberate possibility of paradox, a quality which marks so much of his other work, in architecture, furniture design, and product design, whether through a technique of asking awkward questions or of offering awkward answers.

I used to stay at the Royalton Hotel in New York, in the pre-Starck 1970s and 1980s. It had a friendly, dilapidated feeling. The air conditioners worked only sporadically, and the bathrooms, with their masses of convoluted 1930s pipework, were often slightly bigger than the bedrooms. The TV sets were permanently tuned to a dire soap opera, and there were strange lines on the carpets. These last two I found were related: one morning when I stayed in my room, the maid arrived. Oblivious of my presence, she turned on the television to her favorite soap and proceeded to vacuum the room according to the pattern of lines, never losing sight of the screen. The alternatives to the Royalton were shabby and grim or pompous and pretentious.

The Royalton was Starck's first hotel design, in 1988, and his first association with Ian Schrager. Since then the two of them have extended the definition of the contemporary hotel. Schrager and his partner Steve Bell (who died in 1989) had achieved fame (and a certain subsequent notoriety) as the creators of Studio 54, the hippest club in New York in the 1980s. A few years later they turned their attention to the hotel business, buying first the old Executive Hotel in Manhattan, renaming it Morgans and inviting Andrée Putmann to design the interior. The Royalton, also in Manhattan, was their next project—Schrager had seen illustrations of Starck's work on the Café Costes, and went to

Hotels

see him. What impressed Schrager, as he said in a later interview, "were two things: firstly, Starck was able to take a traditional French *bistro*, move it into the next century, and still maintain its essence. Secondly, he took the bathroom and reinvented it." Since then they have worked on a series of hotels across the United States, including the Paramount in New York, the Delano in Miami, and the Mondrian in Los Angeles. In 1999 two more hotels will open in London. All have been successful; each is different. Schrager dislikes the term "designer hotels"; as he said in an interview, "Our hotels in some way capture a certain time and spirit, and manifest a certain thing about the culture around us." And the hotels' cachet is not just about celebrity. "You want people who want something fresh and original to come to your particular place, people who seek out what's on the edge. Some of the people are celebrities and some are taste-makers, some have money and some don't."

This is achieved by getting both the public and the private spaces of the hotel right, which is the focus of all the Starck-Schrager designs. At the Royalton a narrow lobby had extended from the 44th Street entrance through to 43rd Street. This has been widened, lined with columns, and flanked by a restaurant and bar. While not spacious, it is busy. The Paramount enjoys a larger, square central lobby, reached by a canted staircase—a quite different solution, more

about making an appearance than grazing through. Each of the three elevators at the Paramount is lit internally in a different color.

Schrager agrees that a theatrical approach, which worked well for nightclubs, underlies the public spaces of the hotels. "They have the same purpose: a customer should be treated with respect, and everything done to make sure he or she has fun and so wants to come back. It's the "hospitality business." This is achieved partly by the overall décor and ambience, and partly by identifying and executing the right level of detail. "Having a room with one hundred great ideas is not as important as having a good room," Schrager points out. "Editing and making it all come together is the difficult part. Too many good ideas is as bad as too many poor ideas."

Starck's endless attention to detail and his delight in creating a successful surprise make him an ideal hotel designer. Gérard Garouste has told the story of going for a long walk with Starck through fields and woods in Burgundy. After wondering where they were, Garouste found a bottle of iced champagne waiting for them in a glade. Starck extends this lost-and-found principle to hotels. As he once said, "Being away from home is disorienting for hotel guests, but after settling them down, we want to give them pleasure with mental and visual jokes. If people look closely, they

can discover the secret life and relationship between objects. I call them open symbols." These symbols include a single green apple (the only note of color) on a wall sconce in the bedrooms at the Delano, small guardian angel figurines in the rooms at the Mondrian, books and pictures on the floor of the plain rooms at the Paramount (like an artist's room—a poor artist but a quirky and eclectic one), or a sign on the Mondrian bathroom mirrors saying "me." The same attention to detail applies to the public spaces: a wall of rosebuds at the Paramount, sofas with projecting backs for the Royalton, a flowerpot garden at the Mondrian, high white curtains in the Delano entrance terrace, opening to a dark, cherry-wood-paneled lobby.

While a shared approach and design philosophy that unite client and designer run through the group of hotels, each solution is specific to its location. Their work sends a message to the corporate, look-alike approach of other hotel chains. If Morgans was a stylized hotel that retained its 1930s and 1940s furniture, the Royalton had to have new, contemporary furniture. The Delano avoids the pastel clichés of Miami style while reflecting the contrast between the relaxed tropical setting and the vibrant, bustling city. At the Mondrian, the laid-back naturalness native to California is balanced by its location in the world capital of the movie business. New hotels in the design stage at

the time this is written include an "urban spa" for younger guests in New York, and interactive concepts for the hotels in London. Given the success of their collaboration over the last decade, whatever Starck and Schrager choose to do next will be worth seeing.

"For me," Starck explains, "a hotel is like a beacon, sending out signals of friendship. It is also a wonderful forum for demonstrating, through use, some hints, some gestures, some examples of a way of living that fits in with my ideas, that express them. A visual surprise here, or an architectural feature used in a new way there, even a way of laying out a table, can suggest to people using the hotel new ways of thinking about their own lives. So they leave the hotel thinking, 'That was a nice touch, I'll try that at home.' " If this sounds exaggerated, its effect is nonetheless backed up by guest responses, not only on surveys, but also from the numerous telephone calls Schrager's organization and the hotels themselves get asking for information about details of the hotel décor and services (at one time they had a full-time team answering such calls). "A hotel is simply a school, a permanent school, for showing people how they can live more happily," says Starck.

The same qualities of detail, welcome, and theatricality can be found in Starck's restaurant designs. One of the classic

kamples of this is the Felix restaurant at the Peninsula Hotel in Hong Kong. Even if you are the first person to arrive or dinner, the room appears full. A tribe awaits you, their faces printed in black on the white upright cushions of the hairs around each table. The tribe is Starck's: the faces are those of Starck himself, his daughter Ara, his fiancée atricia, her assistant Laurence, friends such as Christian Mercier or Azucena Camano, and others. As a gesture of elcome, it is disturbing and astonishing, an echo of the designer's continuing involvement in the setting and cenario he has created. Some might consider marking his territory in this way to be an egotistical gesture, but it is ot. The faces invite the guests in.

tarck designed the Felix in 1991, following a series of earlier restaurants including the Manin in Tokyo, the Teatron Mexico City, and the Teatriz in Madrid. The earlier restaurants had the vigorous, almost baroque enthusiasm of his arly club designs, or concert halls such as La Cigale in Paris. Both the Mexico City and Madrid restaurants used, as heir name's imply, **theatrical settings,** with ramps and stairs, curtains and gantries that placed the diner almost terally "on stage." The same strength of gesture is evident at the Peninsula, but with a different expression. It is less emonstrative and more participatory.

The mail-order business in France, as with Sears, Roebuck in the United States, began in the nineteenth century, when manufacturers in St. Etienne in central France realized that many of their customers were a long way away. Their *Catalogue des manufactures des cycles et armes* sold bicycles and pen knives, hunting rifles and zinc buckets all over France. A new impetus was given to this market by the generation born during and after World War II, when the increasingly centralized government could send its employees—teachers and administrators, tax inspectors and museum curators, freshly qualified from the Grands Ecoles—to work anywhere in France. What had been a rural market became younger and more sophisticated. The Trois Suisses group, one of the largest mail-order operations in France, realized this and began to activately promote the work of young designers, including Starck. This project was always important to the president of the company, who in the 1980s and 1990s commissioned special work for the catalogue from young designers. Today there is a Trois Suisses Foundation, which gives grants and scholarships to young designers in different fields to enable them to develop their work.

Many of the first objects by Starck marketed by the Trois Suisses were chairs and tables, often supplied in kit form. In the 1990s, two new projects, each with a wider political edge, appeared. One was the ONF table. The ONF (Office

Mail Order

National des Forêts) is the French national forestry service, created in the late seventeenth century. (Today France has more forest than any other Western European country.) To interest people in conserving and protecting forests, Starck designed a dining table, console table, and bench in clear varnished beech, supported by a raw log from a local forest. A customer would order a table, for example, and then contact the forestry service, who would select a suitable log, fix a numbered seal on it in the buyer's presence, and the table would be complete. (In fact, the table would not stand without the log!) The customer had not only a new table but a day out in a local forest as well. Choosing the table connected the buyer to the forester's world: a double purpose in a single object.

The other project was the complete Starck/Trois Suisses house, launched in 1994. For 5,000 francs (about $1,000), the customer got a complete set of plans for a single-story, freestanding house to be built in wood, complete specifications for timber, plumbing, and wiring, an instructional video, and a hammer. Secondary and holiday homes are popular in France, where land prices outside the main cities are low, and many families have kept in contact with the part of France their ancestors came from. The creation of a new or renovated building above a certain size requires the signature of an architect, with the attendant additional costs and the complexities of local planning

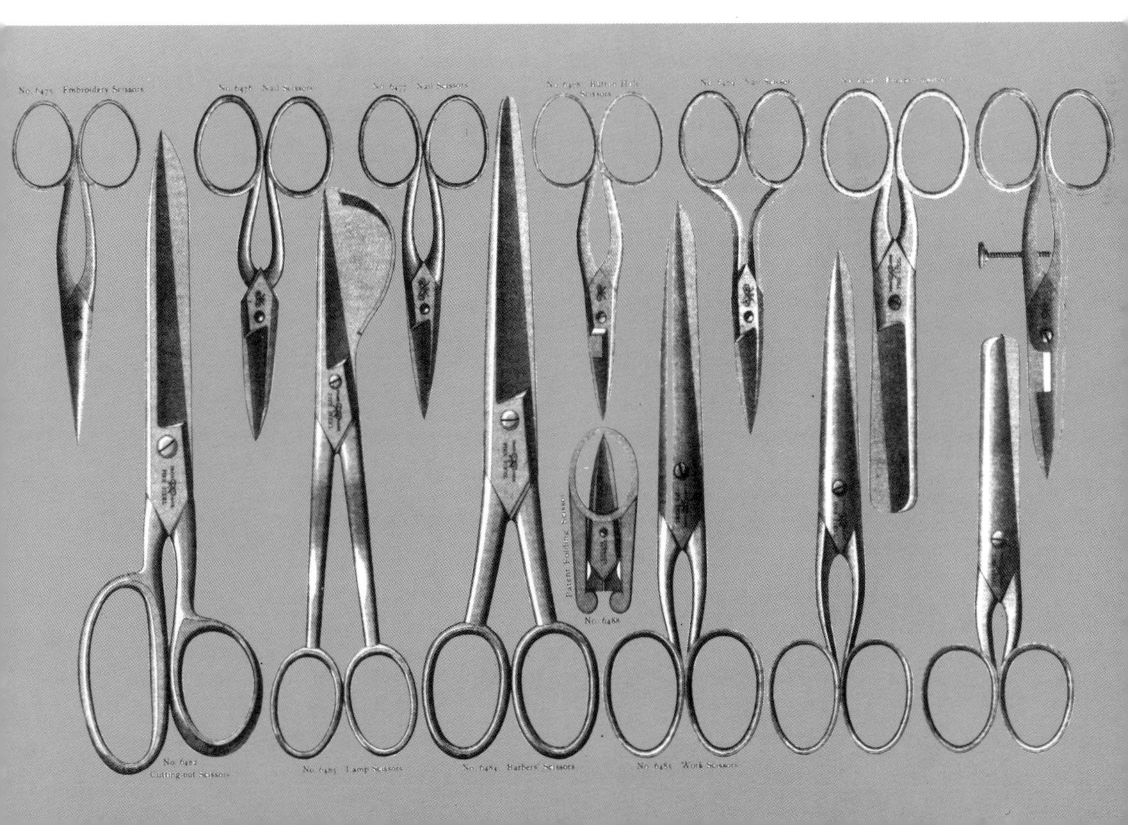

rules. The alternative was to use one of the kit houses or standard plans offered by a number of firms. The latter rarely have any serious design content, which is why ersatz Swiss chalets or imitation Breton cottages have sprung up all over France. Starck's project was for a square house with verandas and a low, pitched roof. It was designed to be appropriate anywhere, in the countryside or by the sea. It was a modern alternative to the derivative historical designs sold by the commercial companies, and at the same time made maximum use of the available space under the planning regulations, which made it straightforward to build. Details such as the exterior finish, color of timber, and interior floorings, and, to a certain extent, the arrangement of room spaces, were left to the consumer, allowing some customization.

Thus the Trois Suisses house is another example of Starck's intervention in a situation where he perceived the competition to be inadequate, or to exclude a certain section of society who did not want or could not afford the services of an architect. It uses the weaknesses of the planning system in an almost subversive way, while offering choice to the public. It is an example of his use of *aikido*, using an opponent's strength so that the opponent defeats himself. The planning system allows you to build up to a certain size without an architect's plan, so the Starck plan

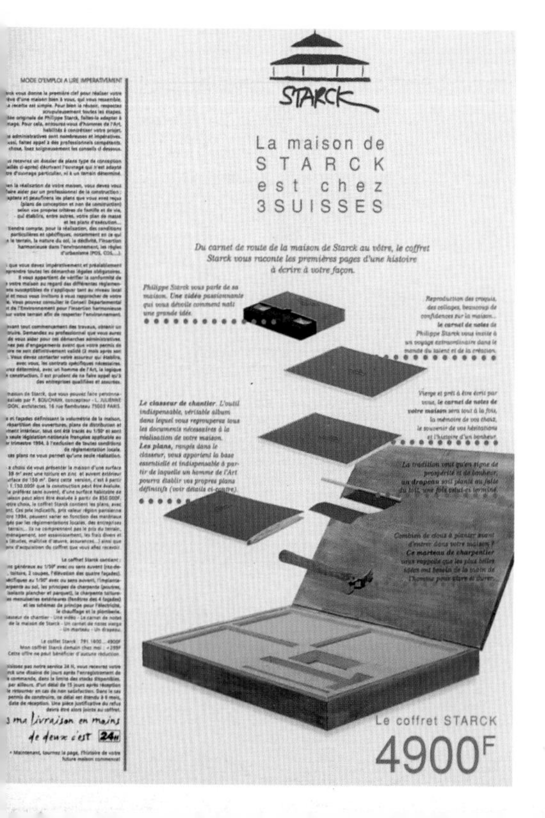

is one square meter short of that limit. The result is also a kind of social balance: you still need planning permission to build—to control overall building density—but you do not have to go through the challenge of working with an architect. You know what you are going to get from the start—you even have a free hammer to start the work with! But society as a whole does not suffer from bad building or inappropriate densities.

As Starck put it in a lecture, "My feeling was that it was wholly unforgivable that people who had some inkling of how they could live better did not have the possibility or the choice to do so, whether we are talking about young people starting off in life who have to accept what they can find, or older people who have spent their lifetimes working to buy houses that are worthless, without affection, without culture, without quality." It is worth noting that one of Starck's favorite homes on the Meditteranean island of Formentera is one of these Trois Suisses designs. (He has a number of different homes, in France and elsewhere, though the story that each has his favorite motorbike sitting outside it, all working on the same key, is a myth, albeit one Starck at one time let circulate.) It is also the case that the main floor of his office-cum-house at Issy-les-Moulineaux follows the same proportions and layout as the Trois Suisses house.

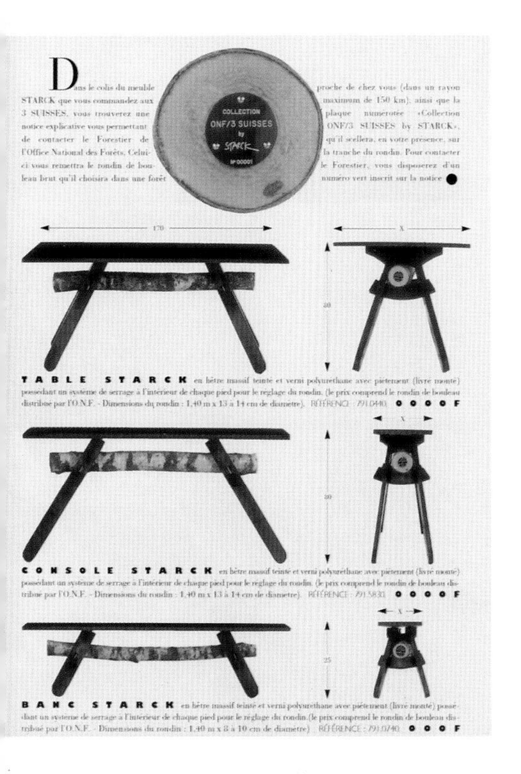

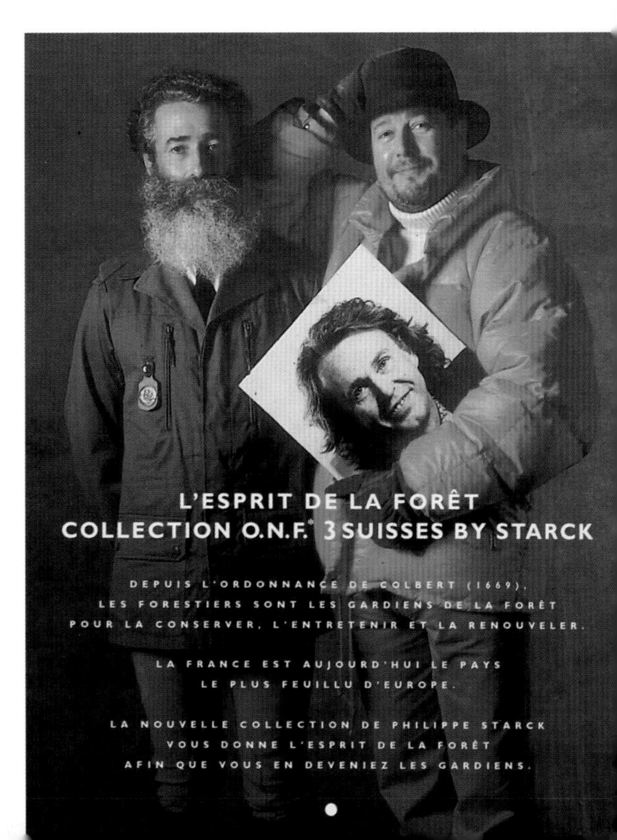

The Milan Furniture Fair, the annual Salone del Mobile, is the design event of the year, every year. For five days in April the city is invaded by design students, journalists, and groupies, by furniture collectors and buyers from all over the world. Not only in the pavilions of the fairground itself, but in shops and galleries and public spaces all over the city, there are exhibitions of furniture. The event—or series of events—takes place on two levels. In most of the pavilions, serious furniture dealers are negotiating discounts on Louis XV television consoles; owners of grand restaurants are testing the pile on the velvet of ever-larger dining chairs; and managers of garden centers are enthusiastically examining marble-finish outdoor tables in weatherproof plastic. That is the proper fair: serious business for an important Italian industry. The other fair is a maelstrom of small exhibitions and presentations of ideas and concepts, minimalist and high-tech, back to nature or backs to the wall, romanticized or politicized, from designers in the United States, France, Britain, Germany, Holland, Scandinavia, South America, Southeast Asia, and Japan. Bridging the gap between the two are a small group of Italian companies that have embraced the concept of contemporary furniture and design and are trying to bring it to a world market, companies such as Kartell and Cassina, Flos and Artemide, Baleri and Alessi. They are growing in number, with established markets in Italy, Germany, and the United States. It is

in part because these companies are represented at the fair that students, beginners, and hopefuls come to show their work. An order for a chair or table from an established company can launch a career.

They also come for the parties, the gossip, and the news. Certain Salone events are legendary, such as the launch of Memphis in 1981, which put furniture back at the top of the design agenda with grace, wit, and extraordinary zest. Others are regular moments, anticipated from one year to the next: Ron Arad and Ingo Maurer's joint exhibition of sculptural furniture and beautiful lamps, the Dutch group Droog Design's simple, subtle, and witty evocations of the world of materials, Alessandro Mendini's adventures wih color, or Rolf Sachs's minimalist explorations of form. There is also the annual lecture in the Palazzo del Triennale, given in 1998 by Philippe Starck. The speech had to be relayed by loudspeakers to the park outside, as even the largest hall was full, and at the end it took four bodyguards to get Starck out through the throng.

In 1980 Starck set up Ubik to market his own furniture designs, since the French manufacturers he had approached had rejected him. His early products included the 1977 Easilight, a fluorescent tube fitted with black rubber ends that could be hung from the ceiling or simply leaned against a wall (as could the 1981 lamp Soudain le Sol Trembla, a

baseball bat with lampshade). Among the early chairs were Dr. Bloodmoney, a 1977 canvas and metal kit chair named after a Philip K. Dick character, and the 1972 Joe Miller folding chair, which used a precursor to the three-legged system employed for the Café Costes chair. The products never made much money. "I never was very good at business," Starck now says, "never having learned any mathematics. And the quality control on the early furniture was awful, as I made them all myself!" But help was at hand, from two sources.

One was VIA, an independent body set up by the French government and furniture industry in 1979 to promote new design talent at home and abroad. VIA organized a French presence at trade fairs internationally, and each year gave selected young designers carte blanche to create a series of prototype designs that would be exhibited internationally. In 1981 one of the designers they chose was Philippe Starck. The Dole Melipone table in steel and granite was among the designs he created, as was the Al Hammond bookcase.

The other initiative came from a chance meeting. In 1980 Arturo del Punta was working as director of a Franco-Italian design company with a showroom opposite the Pompidou Center in Paris: Starck was creating offices for a graphic designer in the same building and showed his projects to del Punta, who agreed to present them to Italian companies

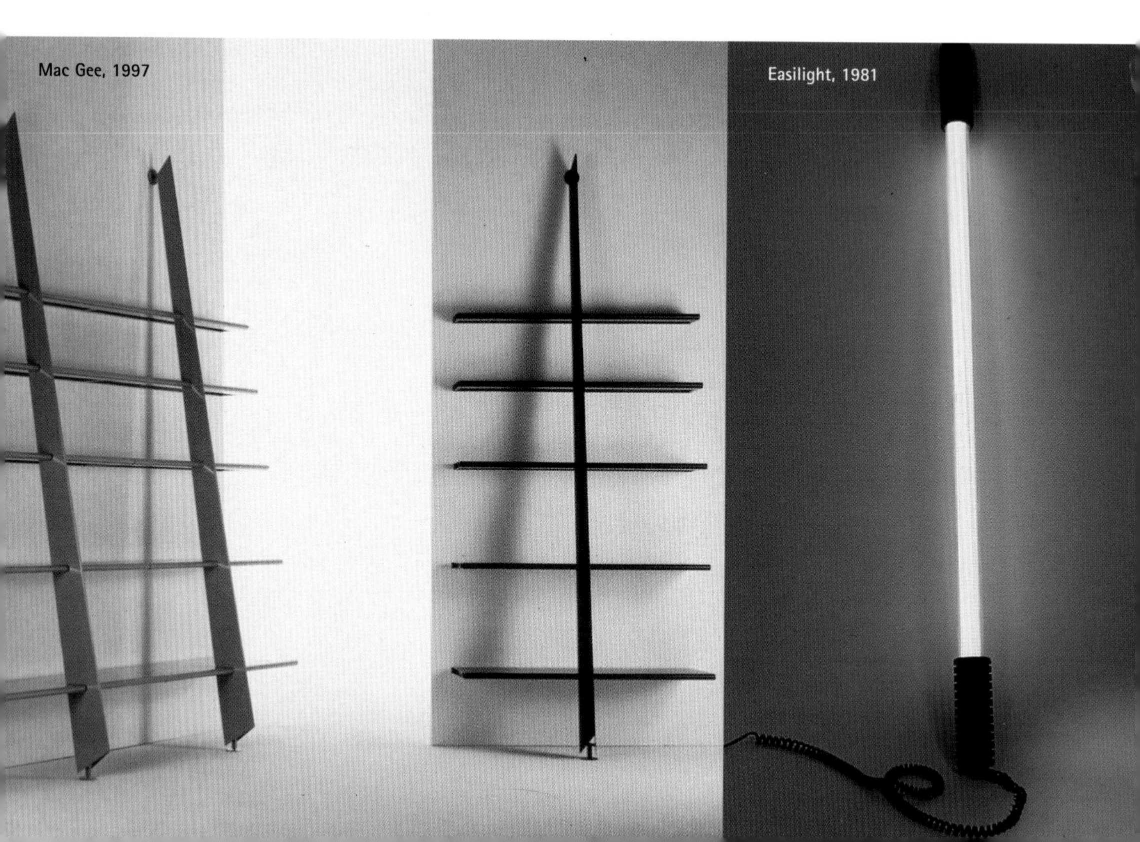

Mac Gee, 1997

Easilight, 1981

on his next trip. "I had a lot of refusals," del Punta said in a 1998 interview, "until I went to see Baleri. Three days later the head of Baleri went to Paris to sign a contract with Starck. The problem with genius, I realize, is how to convince others of it. The genius is always a long way ahead of the rest. Starck has a remarkable understanding of the psychology of his products, and on a personal level he is an unusual man who has immense respect for people, whatever their social status. The only thing he doesn't accept is stupidity."

The Baleri contract led to the commercialization of the Francesca Spanish folding chair, the Mac Gee bookcase, and the Richard III armchair, used in the Elysée apartments. It assured Starck of a presence in Milan, and helped him to international fame as a furniture designer, just as the commission for the Elysée Palace had brought him to the forefront of interior design. Most of his furniture design is still for and through Italian companies, notably Kartell, Cassina/Driade, and Flos, though he also works with the French company XO.

Starck's strategy as a furniture and product designer is based on **anonymity, ambivalence, and choice.** Anonymity in two senses: his design is not about personal aesthetic statements, about saying "Starck made me!"; rather, his designs emerge from a series of reflections on non-design issues—technology and materials, human behavior, and society. As

Soudain le sol trembla, 1981

he said in a 1980 interview, "In that thousands of perfectly valid versions of most pieces of furniture exist, a new work must of necessity be symbolic. This symbolism is directly linked to social life, to material technology and to production methods." From this perspective the designer is not creating but responding; the design arises from the anonymous needs of society, even if it is mediated by the designer's personal decision to intervene.

Ambivalence is a consequence of anonymity: it emerges from the furniture's role as both sign and signifier, as medium and message. Take the Richard III chair. From the front it looks like a traditional club armchair: high, rounded arms, deep seat, full back. But look behind it, and the rest has, literally, gone: the bulky corners of the back are replaced by a single thin curve ending in a single foot. There are various levels of explanation for this. Starck once pointed out that "you always found club armchairs sitting on pavements when you came out of nightclubs at dawn. All that solid bourgeois comfort, out on the street." The idea of the bourgeoisie disposing of their symbolic accoutrements under the cover of darkness has a certain discrete charm. Partly it was a problem of size: club chairs were designed for spaces more ample than the average Parisian apartment. But also the society using the chairs had changed, had mutated. Heavy leather comfort was no longer the right representation. How then to create the comfort of the club chair in the

Ceci n'est pas une brouette, 1996

right terms? By using technology to save space and weight, and by mutating the form into something completely modern. It becomes, as Starck said, "a dialectical game about topology and social representation. It has lost the connotations of a club chair, but still is one." If there is an ambiguity in this, that is the necessary concomitant to social change.

The third element is choice. Creating opportunities for people to choose is central for Starck. He sees any form of elitism as social theft. "You must shake people up, say to them, 'Take an interest in your life.' If I carry on working, though I don't need to, it's solely because I feel I have a duty to bring some pleasure, some happiness, to others." Anonymity, ambivalence, and choice inform not only his furniture design. They are also valid in his housewares for Alessi, and in the program for Thomson to redesign their complete range of consumer electronics. His architectural work shares the same qualities of comprehension and confrontation. For example, in the new recycling plant currently under construction at Vitry, just outside Paris, he has deliberately set aside the conventional iconography of the factory in favor of a white, amorphous but monumental shape. For Starck, designing in a new way, appropriate to an age in mutation, means continuous self-criticism, auto-subversion, and social awareness.

Louis XX, 1988

ff1600

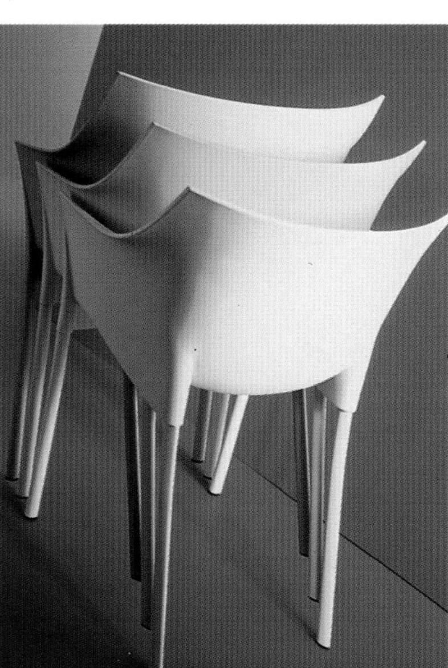

Dr. No, 1996

ff695

La Marie, 1998

ff400

Recent archaeological research suggests that making flint hand-axes was not simply a method of creating tools, but also part of a wider cultural system that enabled men to show themselves as competent flintsmiths and so worthy to mate with their choice of females. Future archaeologists may be drawn to similar conclusions about chair design in the twentieth century. Sufficient ways of keeping the human body off the ground had been devised in earlier centuries, they will argue a couple of millennia hence, so there must be some explanation other than necessity for so many different designs appearing in the short period between 1950 and 2000. And in a sense they will be right. Designing a chair has become something of a rite of passage for furniture designers, a means of establishing their independent positions, their places. Think of a designer, and you think of a chair: Mies van der Rohe's Barcelona chair, Charles and Ray Eames's molded plywood lounge, Alessandro Mendini's Proust, to take three examples. Each makes a fairly clear statement about the design philosophy of the maker, and you can use the chairs created by a particular designer as a set of marker posts for his design development.

The same is true for Starck, except that in his case there is an important additional factor: the retail price of the chair. Most designers expect the prices for their work to rise as they become more established and well known—a wholly

Chairs

reasonable return on their investment of knowledge and energy. Jean Nouvel once wryly described his furniture designs to me as a pension fund that would keep generating a royalty income for him if he ever stopped designing buildings. Not so Starck. He has used his position in the market to reduce the retail price of his chairs. Price-cutting is known business practice, but this was not Starck's motive: the idea came from his concept of the chair itself.

"A chair should look like everything and nothing," he said, "by which I mean that you should think you recognize it when you see it for the first time. They are among the objects I think of as 'anonymous-plus'—they emerge from a collective unconscious." Starck's design process is not about individual expression but about engaging with this unconscious. If his starting point is interpreting this archetype, "finding a form that expresses communal memory," his end point is governed by wider considerations, particularly his desire to offer people both choice and opportunity. Choice requires a range of products; opportunity involves affordability. It was not only a policy of idealism, for Starck had the intuition that it would work in the market. The Dr. No chair, for example, has sold very well for Kartell. Similarly, the Bubu stool range, first launched in 1991, has been regularly expanded with different colors and a complementary product, Prince Aha, which can be used in different color combinations as "an exercise in liberty," as Starck says.

Lord Yo, 1994

In the mid-1990s Starck produced a series of designs for beds for Cassina in Italy with names such as Soeur Jeanne or Soeur Marie. One American magazine proclaimed that these were in memory of the nuns who had been his schoolteachers in his formative years. But Starck's use of names is not so obvious.

Starck's naming of his products and furniture designs presents a curious pattern. Almost all are named in English (the Cassina beds are an exception). A number of names, especially for early pieces, such as Dr. Bloodmoney, come from Philip K. Dick's work, as did the title of Starck's second business, Ubik. There is a certain assonance between Starck's morbid, even suicidal view of the world and Dick's brilliantly skewed vision of **future worlds,** with its dark and absurd undertones and its elevation of objects to ritual vehicles of cult memory. Sometimes this concept is at the heart of his stories, as in "The Days of Perky Pat." In one of his major novels, *The Man in the High Castle*, the main subplot concerns the development of a series of objects that will define American culture under Japanese-German occupation, after the United States loses World War II.

But just as it is clear from *The Man in the High Castle* that the setting may be real or parallel, a construct of real events or of the I-Ching, it makes no sense to take Starck's names for his products as single realities; rather, we

Naming

should see them as ambitious paradoxes. Paradoxes first in why a French designer should so often choose English names for his products; second, in that almost all of his namings consist of name-plus-title (Dr. No, Lord Yo, Miss Tripp, for example) while he is always called Starck, even by those who have worked with him for years; and third, why names at all, given the addiction to numbers and acronyms that make up the coded language of so much modern technology?

Naming is ambitious because Starck is perfectly aware that naming an object, like naming a child, is a ritual that endows it with its **own personality.** The strange shiny thing on the kitchen table is "my Juicy Salif," not "Starck's lemon squeezer." Starck explains that by being named and known, objects and things enter into our consciousness, and so merit our care and remind us of our duty of love. Choosing an unusual or even quirky name reinforces this process, as does indulging in wit and humor. In choosing names Starck not only makes literary allusions; he honors friends and family, members of his "tribe," such as his daughter Ara and son Oa, and indulges in his taste for onomatopoeia, like the Hot Bertaa kettle or the Dadada stool. Through their affection and amusement, the names of his products reach out to bring the user into the wider human family.

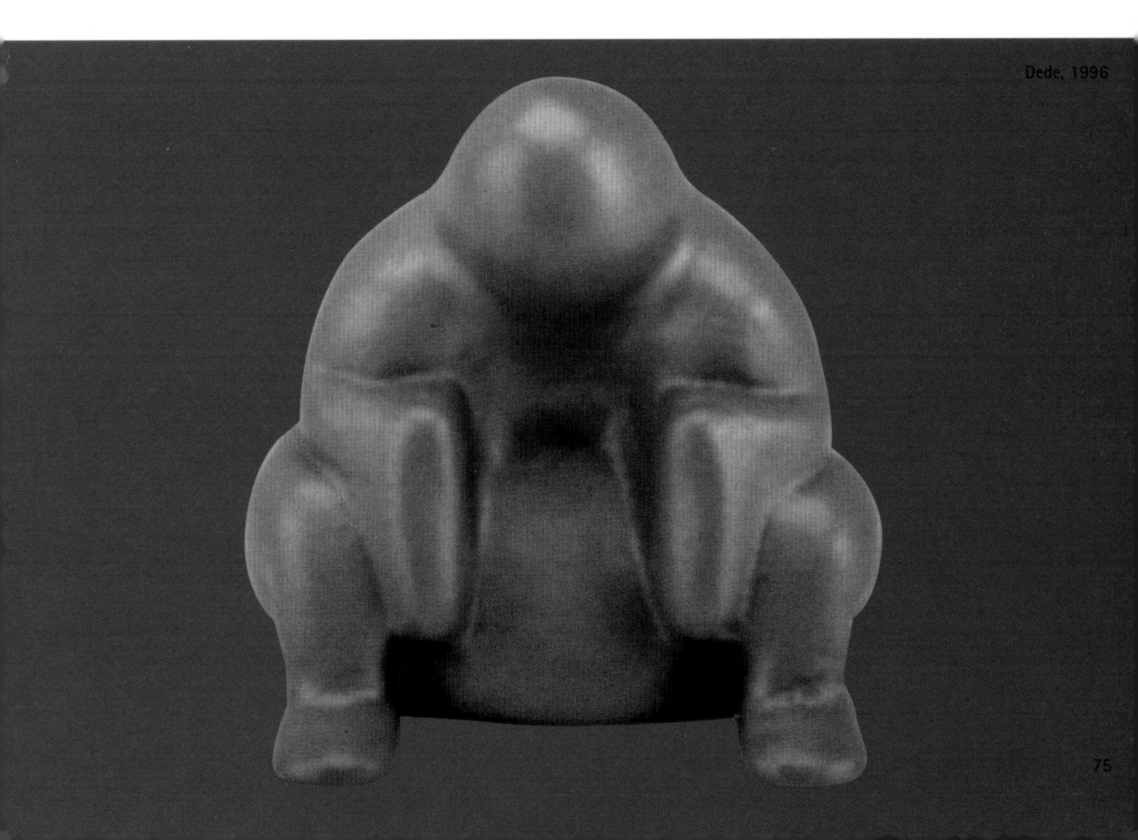

Dede, 1996

How does one reanimate the modern home? The technology revolution has introduced a whole register of new communication and information systems, yet it tends to promote isolation: people don't surf the net as a family. Microwaveable instant food means teenagers eat meals at their own times. With a Walkman you listen to music individually. How do you re-create a family space within a family home? The Neos and LWS collections address this problem.

Starck, not surprisingly, thought big. The Neos sofa is the size of a double bed, with high arms and backs: a family nest, almost, with room for many. The round Neos table is as high as a bar. Like a bar, you can use it standing or seated, at the right level. "These are deliberately bourgeois products," Starck explains, "with the comfortable values of bourgeois furniture." But adapted for today's needs: parents can dine formally at the table while the children stand and snack. It is not only an alternative to the standard dining table, it offers further choices as well. "The table," as Starck puts it, "is about communication. It means that two generations can talk to each other."

"I also designed these projects as a challenge to what I myself had achieved so far. I'd created the success of the inexpensive plastic chair and taken it about as far as it could go, and everyone had followed me, so it was time to turn

Work Space

around. I became my own target. When an idea dominates a market or a situation, you have to subvert it, even if the idea is your own. Knowing, of course, that the idea is going to survive, it is simply no longer going to dominate. It's not the first time I've done this," he explains with glee, "and it won't be the last!" So he turned to expensive, solid furniture for the middle classes. "Don't let's be racist—the bourgeoisie have their problems too. And for me there was nothing more to say about simple chairs." The Lazy Work Sofa is simply a very large sofa, deep and comfortable, with tables that clip onto the arms or back, and with fittings for lights. "My idea," Starck explains, "was that if you have a sofa big enough for all the family to sit on or around, then you create an island that people can come to, instead of splitting away to different places to do different things. The wage-earner realizes here a space for working at home rather than in some detestable office. His or her partner can have a workspace on the other side, and the whole family can pile onto it at the weekend to watch a video or play a game. It is a deliberate nonproduct. To create it I simply looked at all the designs for existing comfortable sofas on the market and made an amalgam of them, so that the result would have as little personality as possible. For that reason it would work, as a way of encouraging people to be together, to share love. Because it starts out anonymous, you can add your own ideas to it."

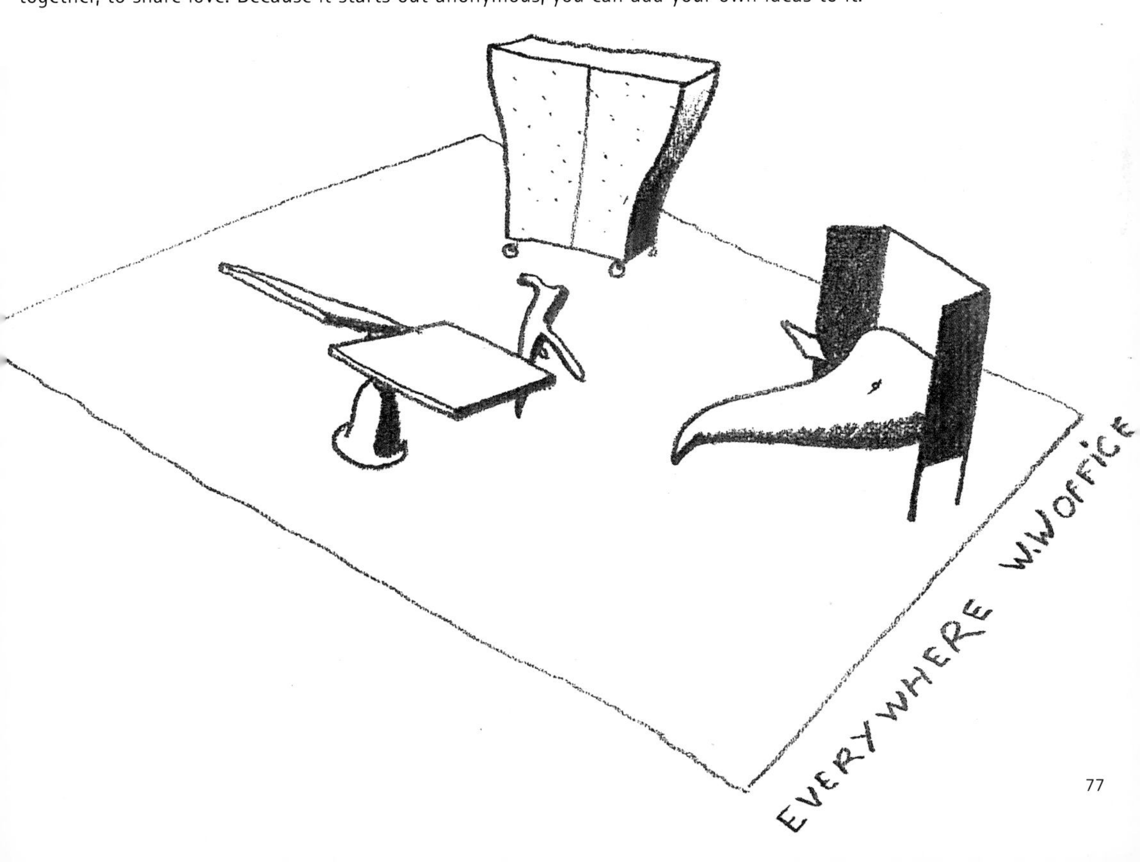

Alberto Alessi's grandfather left the family village high in the Piedmontese mountains in northwestern Italy to set up a metal-forming and -cutting works in the valley below, by the side of Lake Orca; his son Carlo—Alberto's father—studied industrial design and took over the direction of the factory in 1945. Alberto wanted to study philosophy or architecture; his father wanted him to be an economist. They compromised on law. Alberto Alessi joined the family firm in 1970 as commercial director, but twenty years later he passed that role on to his younger brother and devoted himself to design and communication, subjects that had always passionately interested him and which had formed a growing part of Alessi's business since their first coffeemakers, produced in the 1950s.

Since then, the success of Alessi in the design world has been intense. They have created not only new collections featuring the work of leading designers from around the world every year, but also a positive interest in the work of young designers, through either the continuing work of the Alessi Research Center in Milan or specific events, such as the Family Follows Fiction workshop in 1993. That workshop heralded Alessi's move from primarily metalwork objects to an interest in plastics and a new product iconography based on Pop Art, comic books, and cartoons.

The Alessi achievement developed out of a *fabrica*, an Italian term for a system that combines the concern for

Icons

personality and quality of craft with the convenience of machine-based production. As Michele de Lucchi pointed out to me, the strength of the furniture and design business in Milan relies in part on the existence of such *fabricche*, which provide a skills base for creating prototypes and short-run productions in a whole range of disciplines and materials. It is a system that creates flexibility and opportunity for an enlightened marketplace.

Alessi's success still has deeper roots. Alberto Alessi calls his approach to design "SMI," Sensoriality, Memory, Imagination. This approach looks for **affective codes** in objects and uses the forms of objects to evoke unconscious memories and desires, which in turn often have a narrative structure.This approach relates design to fiction more than poetry, if one seeks a parallel among literary genres. It represents a delicate balance that mass production can almost never attain (and rarely seeks) since it is driven by cost, not concept. Occasionally it achieves this balance—the Citroen DS is a classic example, though from the 1950s. More recently, the British Airways World Images identity created by Newell & Sorrell attained the same level of subtle charm. A Ndebele painting, a Chinese calligraphic pattern, or a Polish folk-art image evokes the adventure and mystery of flying, rather than the solid, terrestrial corporate values offered by other airlines.

Ara, 1988

Through the concept of the *fabrica* and SMI, Alberto Alessi is describing quite simply an intelligent and intellectual investment in industrial production. As Alessi has claimed in the book that accompanied the Family Follows Fiction collection, there is a direct link to the traditions of the English Arts and Crafts movement and the Wiener Werkstatte. His insistence on the narrative also is crucial. Mass production offers conscious narrative, as in the Princess Diana memorial object, the World Cup souvenir. However important (or not) the events narrated by such objects, the narrative is conscious, and thus replaced rapidly in the conscious mind by later events. Designs that appeal to the subconscious or unconscious **narrative memory** not only have a longer life and a wider application, they also fulfill a wider and deeper purpose. The designs Alessi described funtion in 1994 as "Helping to fulfill, through the paradoxical, creative dimension of our products, people's desire to be a little happier."

There are evident correlations here between Starck's thinking and Alessi's, like the appeal to the unconscious and the desire to spread human happiness through design. In the Family Follows Fiction essay, Alessi commented on Starck's work: "And what about the work of Philippe Starck? When I think of the reiterated use of the horn icon, or of such enigmatic, ambiguous—yet so keenly desired—objects as the Juicy Salif lemon squeezer and the Mr. Meu-Meu cheese

Puzzle, 1987

grater, it seems clear to me that 'Beauty' is the wrong word to describe them, and that a more appropriate one should be looked for in the zone of 'Perturbation-Uneasiness-Fear.' Starck's work even touches certain inner chords that are, in my opinion, associated with the most difficult and 'dangerous' of affective codes; and this makes him a courageous tightrope-walker, grappling with the great mystery of the affections, and in particular with the code of life and death."

That this affective **code of danger** is one of the most difficult to integrate into a collection aimed at adding to the joys of human life has been remarked on by the designer Constantin Boym, among others, who cites the aggressive curves and sharp edges of Starck's designs for Alessi, shown on these pages, as an example. Starck's more recent work for Alessi has both aggression and roundness: the Dr. Skud flyswatter, with its onomatopoeic name and its curious face-on-the-swat design, is proof of the dark forces still at work. What Starck has intuited and Alessi understood is that creating happiness is not just a matter of bright colors and cheerful smiles, fun and useful as that can be. Happiness comes also from a shared knowledge of perils or risks, from the realization that others have faced and understood the same problems.

Royalton stool, 1988

Quatre Etrangeites, 1996

In the early 1990s, European consumer electronics manufacturers were having a hard time. Pressures in the retail market, particularly from Japanese competitors, were pushing prices down, while consumers were demanding more sophisticated technology (with its consequent higher initial costs). Thomson Consumer Electronics, part of a major French group whose interests included microelectronics and military hardware, and whose brand range included Saba, Telefunken, and Brandt, was among the companies suffering. The board appointed Alain Prestat as CEO as part of their solution. He made a number of changes to the operational structure, organized production and branding more coherently, and replanned the marketing and sales system. He also had the design department report directly to him, and in 1992 he invited Starck to a meeting.

The way Starck tells it, Prestat asked him to design a showroom for Thomson in Paris, to which Starck replied with his usual candor that a showroom by him would only emphasize the poor design of Thomson products. By the end of the meeting, they had agreed that Starck would become art director for Thomson, with a free hand to redesign the whole product line. Other consumer electronics companies were also seeing design as a route out of their difficulties: Philips, for example, created a collection with Alessi, Alessandro Mendini as art director. But the makeover at Thomson was to

Home Work

be total: Starck's appointment, given that he had no track record in this area of product design, was radical. To meet the challenge, Starck recruited a new international design team, called Tim Tom, with whom the design credits are shared. (Starck's usual practice is to sign all his designs himself, except for his architectural projects, which are co-signed with the architect.)

Perhaps what interested Starck most about the Thomson proposal was that it opened up the **electronic backbone** of the home to him: the telephone, television, stereo system, and remote controls that make up the entertainment and communication of the family. But it also gave him access to the street, to portable music systems, and so to designing for youth. These two strands can be seen in two of the television sets he designed: Jim Nature for Saba, and Zéo. "When I saw the endless gray and black plastic that televisions are cased in," he explained in a lecture, "I just wanted to show that alternatives were possible. So I used a material I knew well, and made the case from sawdust, glued and formed: that was Jim Nature, and because it was so different it rapidly became a flagship product. The Zéo television was a specific marketing request, a product for young people. I thought that while we watch television upright, kids don't. So I made a television that could sit at an angle as well as upright, so you can watch it lying down."

Ola, 1996

Starck's primary contribution to Thomson consisted of finding more appropriate forms for the existing repertory of products, such as the Hook and To Yoo telephones, the Moa Moa and Moosk radios with their Brancusi shapes, and the Coo Coo alarm clock. Others were more ambitious, such as the Alo soft plastic telephone, which could be personalized by the user, or the Krazy Jacket (a joint venture between Adidas and Saba) with its built-in sound system. Such products tried to extend existing **product semantics** into more communicative areas and away from the control, technology, and power embodied by many electronic consumer products. Thus the Vertigo portable projector uses a natural form as a stand, rather than a formal tripod or frame. One of the most interesting products, from this standpoint, is the Perso video-conferencing unit. Instead of following the logics of a computer screen or a telephone, it deliberately plays down the technology link and is designed as a sort of book, which opens to reveal a "full page" LCD image with the camera for the outgoing image at the top and a speaker and other controls on the facing "page." This presents cutting-edge technology in a non-techno envelope, as is the stereo system Rock'n Rock, which uses an induction system to pass the acoustic signal from the portable stereo unit on top to the amplifier and speakers below. Starck's work for Thomson brought him into contact with the potential impact of technology on everday life in a new

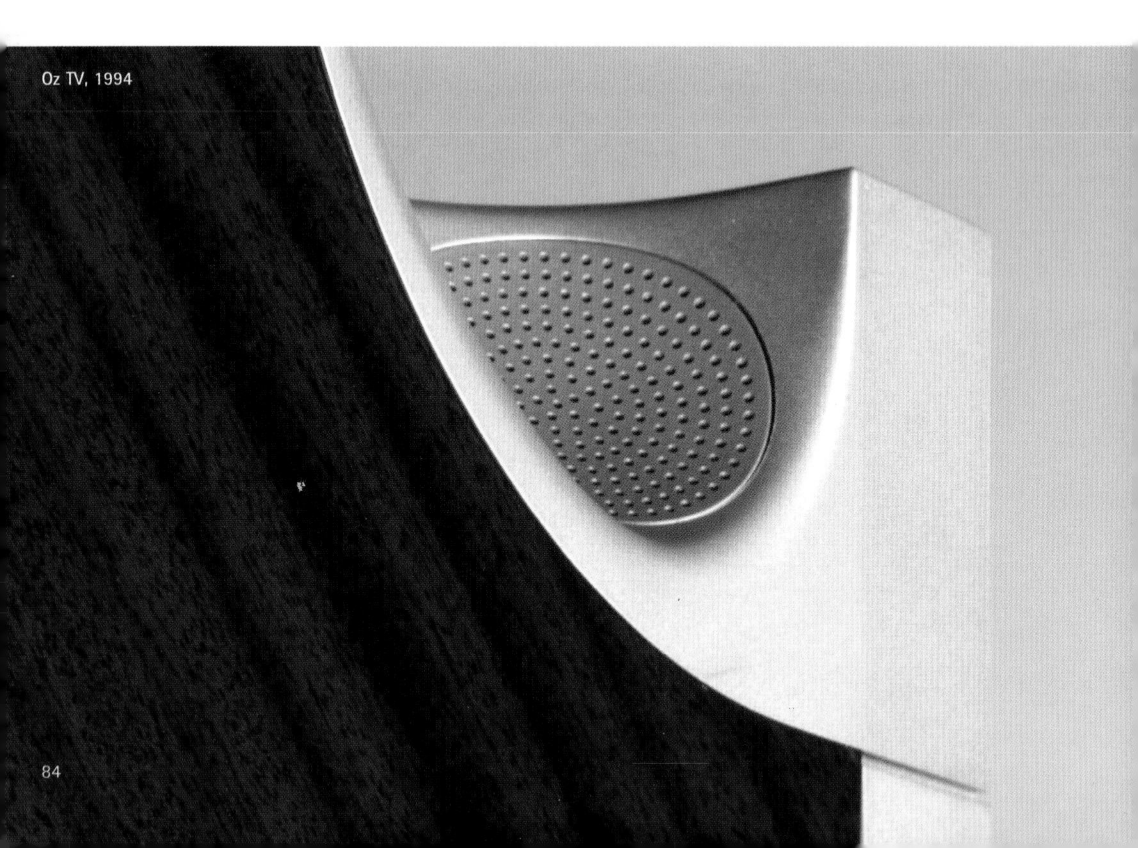

Oz TV, 1994

way. For however broad his previous vision or intentions, most of his earlier projects had been concerned with relatively small markets or with established areas of cultural activity. The invitation from Thomson, through its opportunity and diversity, was an introduction to the realities of the world of mass-production, an opportunity to rewrite the iconography of the everyday. Some business commentators seemed to assume his role would be purely decorative, intervening at the end of the design process to add a touch of color or a fanciful feature. If so, they had overlooked Starck's thoroughness and integrity, and his refusal to compromise once a design decision had been made. That the importance of the opportunity was clear to Starck can be judged from his creation of a new design team for the project, and the implicit realization that a new range of skills, which his existing team did not necessarily have, would be needed. The boldness of his solutions, and the client's willingness to carry many through into production, are proof that Starck's involvement was not simply cosmetic but part of a determined plan to reposition Thomson's product range in terms of a new vision of the relationship between object, consumer, and function. It perhaps could only have been achieved by bringing in, at the top level, a designer who was unfamiliar with the details of the field, who would not be inhibited by past experience and could draw on a broader background and a different perspective.

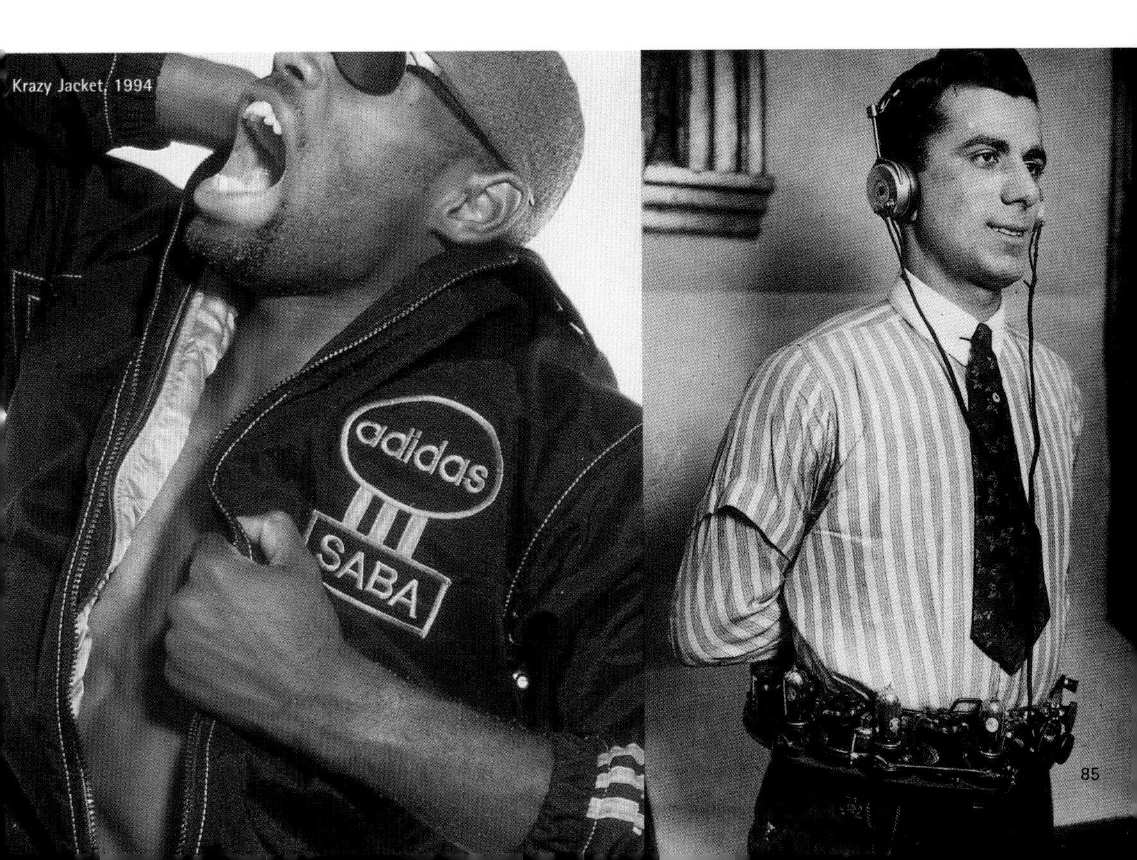

Krazy Jacket, 1994

English design writer Jane Withers once aptly compared Starck to the American industrial designer Raymond Loewy: both are French-born and both have garnered a worldwide audience. Both have an astonishingly broad output and an intuitive sense of the media and its potential for design. But the comparison stops there, not just because of the two generations separating them. Loewy was among the small group who invented, almost by accident, the profession of industrial designer in post-depression America. Unlike other designers of the time, such as Henry Dreyfuss and Walter Dorwin Teague, he saw design in terms of value to the client and not to society. Above all, Loewy saw design as a decorative process, giving the brute object—copier, car, or locomotive—an external form. In October 1949, Loewy appeared on the cover of *Time* magazine under the headline "He Streamlines the Sales Curve."

For all the aesthetic beauty of many of Starck's objects, their appearance is neither a starting point nor a culmination. The dialectics of a Starck design are framed in the social aspects, the political agenda, or the technical challenges the design brief presents. The look of the object derives from these as much as from Starck's **visual sensibilities.** Take the example of the Mikli spectacles and sunglasses. What he found interesting was the engineering task of designing a joint between the main frame and temples that would be entirely flexible, thus making the fit more comfortable for

Products

the wearer, and reducing the risk of damage or breakage. Alain Mikli and Starck eventually developed a joint based on the working of the human clavicle, and it is this elegant aspect of the design that pleases Starck most.

Design led by social, political, and technical issues risks being serious, if not dull, and addressing itself to basic and direct issues, without luxuries. But Starck is happy designing luxury products within his own criteria. While he turned down a commission from Hermès to design a line of luggage for them because the company, despite much goodwill, could not agree to substitute an artificial material for leather, he has also designed luxury sailboats and pleasure boats for Beneteau. As he once said in a lecture, "They do some of the finest work in the world, and it was a privilege to work alongside their craftsmen." In other words, a design strategy that excludes luxury projects simply because they are luxurious is a strategy of denial, and consequently antisocial. Truly antisocial products, such as guns, are excluded because of their nature, not their luxury, while an acceptable product can also be used to convert unacceptable aspects of similar products.

The Aprilia motorcycle is a key example of this. Starck is still an enthusiastic biker (the image on the cover of this book shows him with injuries after a motorcycle accident); since his youth he has always had a motorbike or sports car. The

First 35,7,Voilier L Coque 1992

invitation to design a motorbike, then, must have been almost irresistible. Starck chose to reinvent the iconography of the motorcycle, while at the same time creating an eloquent and elegant object. Out went glaring chrome in favor of brushed steel, in came orange and grey in the place of red and black. The product semantics of the motorbike, so often related to brute power and sheer force, here become balance and grace. The same qualities can be found in his Lama motorscooter and the prototype X Ray 1000 motorbike of 1996.

Starck's willingness to engage with specialized or luxury products seems to contradict his interest in mass-production, shown in his chair design and in his mail-order work with Trois Suisse. But in promoting the greatest good for the greatest number, Starck has avoided the design gesture, the object for the cognoscenti only. Rather, he has chosen to operate on the broadest front, and to accept that responsible design can incorporate responsible pleasure as well, because, as he says, "refusing to accept the reality of pleasure is a refusal to accept the opportunity of love."

Quim Larrea, writing in the Spanish magazine *Ardi* in 1994, commented that "everyone knows about Starck's youthful prowess, the exaggeratedly arrogant profile published a thousand times, and most of all his designs and objects that

Moto 6,5 1995

undoubtedly achieve what they are meant to achieve by raising awkward questions in hitherto unchallenged areas of design." This is certainly true: why should a chair be expensive, or a colander only functional, if they can be made joyful at the same time? But Starck not only raises questions, awkward or otherwise, he also provides solutions that exemplify elegance and opportunity.

The question of what Larrea cites as Starck's "prowess," his ability to move from one field of design to another, raises a fundamental issue about how we perceive Starck. Does a central theme underly his work, or is he using a range of gifts in different ways? The concept of the Renaissance man, able to move between media with Leonardoesque ease, is an attractive one, seen in opposition to the narrow, dedicated specialist. But the Renaissance man concept itself overlooks the fragmentation of contemporary culture by assuming a hegemony that has long disappeared. It is perhaps more appropriate today to compare those who interact with a range of cultural phenomena and those who pursue a single line (a comparison similar to Isaiah Berlin's famous foxes and hedgehogs: "The fox knows many things, but the hedgehog one big thing"). In these terms, Starck is following a certain vision, but by a process of choice and opportunity, rather than by deliberate engagement: a contradictory position, acting as fox but being hedgehog.

X Ray 1000 (Prototype) 1996

Starck's office—the Agence Starck—is on the Ile St. Germain in Issy-les-Moulineaux, on the south bank of the Seine just to the east of Paris. For someone who believes that mutation is inevitable and necessary, it is a good location, a testimonial to change. The office fronts a narrow branch of the Seine, no longer large enough for modern barges, with a jumbled mixture of pleasure boats, houseboats, and old barges, some half sunk, tied up along the opposite bank. Above the riverbank, the concrete piers of a highway carry traffic into Paris. One hundred meters to the west was a series of anonymous modern office blocks adjoining the bridge over the Seine. On the other side of the street are small suburban villas, old and new. To the east are Starck's Le Moult house, then the offices of the advertising agency CLM/BBDO, housed in a fake rusted barge designed by Jean Nouvel, then a modern school with shining playground fittings. The area is a palimpsest of suburban development.

The Agence itself is a square, four-story building, clad in pale pistachio metal. Offices are located on the second and third floors, with Starck's own office overlooking the environs on the top floor. The design studio is in the basement. His office has a dark wooden floor, a large glass-topped desk, sometimes a large bed and a cot for his baby, Oa, sometimes a sofa. On the first floor—linked to the entrance by a walkway, as the site slopes—is a meeting room plus

salon, filled with bibelots and "Starckeries," with Neoz tables and large sofas. It's not quite clear whether it is an office or a home. **The Agence** employs about eight to ten people—modelmakers, designers, graphic artists, architects, and secretaries. It is something of a mixture of a staff and a retinue, for around the core of employees is what Starck calls his "tribe," a group of friends and advisors, companions and consultants, some of whom advise on specific projects, like the architect Luc Arséne-Henry, some of whom work full time, such as Bruno Borrione and Thierry Gaugain. The importance to Starck of such a circle can be seen from the photographs of them that hang outside Starck's own office, but their exact influence cannot be measured.

Starck himself is rarely at the Agence. "This creates a problem," the administrative director, Anne-Marie Grué explained, "as people ring us up to ask for the number of our office in New York, Tokyo, or London. We explain this is the only office. Can they speak to Starck? No, of course not. He really isn't here." Starck travels incessantly to see clients and projects on site, but also to be away, to have time to think. "I'm happiest sitting facing the sea, with a blank page in front of me and an interesting project to work on," he once told me. Being away from the office also avoids the importunities of clients. "I refuse ninety percent of the projects we are offered," he explains, "and on only

one occasion in the last few years have I gone to a client to propose an idea." Given that in 1998 alone the Agence will launch over two hundred new designs, its output is astonishing. Is this genius at high speed? No, it's just sheer hard work.

"When I give the final form to a project I do work fast," Starck admits, "but that's only the final phase of a process of consideration and reflection that can have lasted ten, twenty, even thirty years, during which I have waited for just the right moment. In fact, I have had the same basic preoccupations for a long time, but the time has not always been right for them. If you like, I'm a vicious strategist—not in the sense of vice as evil or mean, but in the sense of a vise as a tool, tenacious, holding firm. Over the years I've unconsciously developed a certain strategic methodology, like Kissinger's small step by small step approach. I take one step, then another. I'm frightened that if I take the wrong step at the wrong time I will lose my effectiveness. Of course sometimes there is a need for urgency, but in general it is better to be slightly slow than to react fast and lose touch. Because if you lose contact you lose the didactic process, the dialogue that feeds a project."

Combine this slow, considered approach with the universal demand for Starck's involvement in all kinds of projects

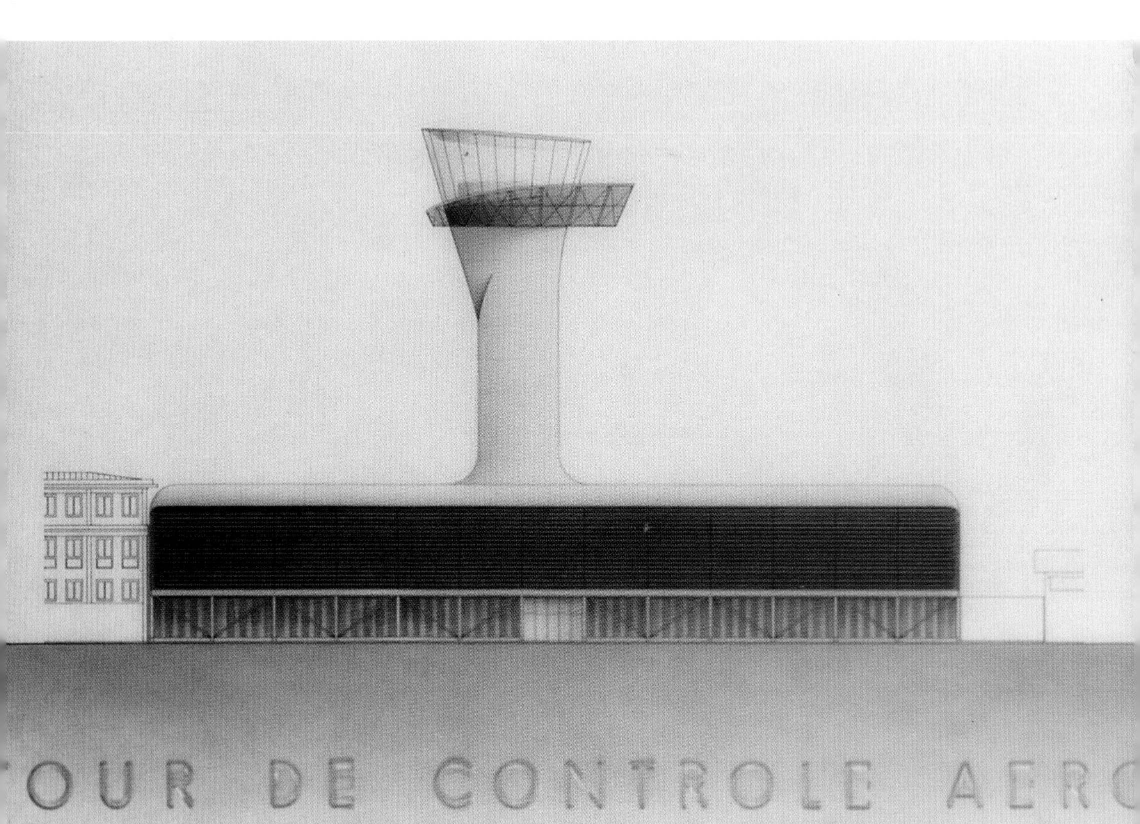

and it opens up a further way of working. "I use a classic left-wing, even Maoist strategy," says Starck, "called 'the enemy within the gates.' Thanks to my present position, itself the result of years of intensive work, most doors are open to me. Many of the people I work with work with me because they want to, because they like my work, and so on. Others see working with me as a potential source of profit (I have no problem with that and they are normally right). This is particularly true of large companies, which have neither much soul nor much instinct, and so seek profit instead. If I accept their invitation, it's not to do them harm—I'm not mischievous like that. But I have my own agenda, and I learn from them about the potential of whatever it is they are doing, and turn it to my own ends—which may often be to their profit as well." The tactic of getting into the enemy camp in disguise is as old as the Trojan horse, but Starck's is an elegant variation, for while he does not share the purposes of the "enemies" he is happy to let them succeed provided he succeeds as well.

The three key new projects for 1998 are the organic foods, OAO, created with Lima; the Good Goods catalogue for the La Redoute mail-order company; and a series of basic goods for the 7-11 shop chain in Japan. These all show Starck moving from his traditional areas of furniture and product and interior design into new fields—foods and

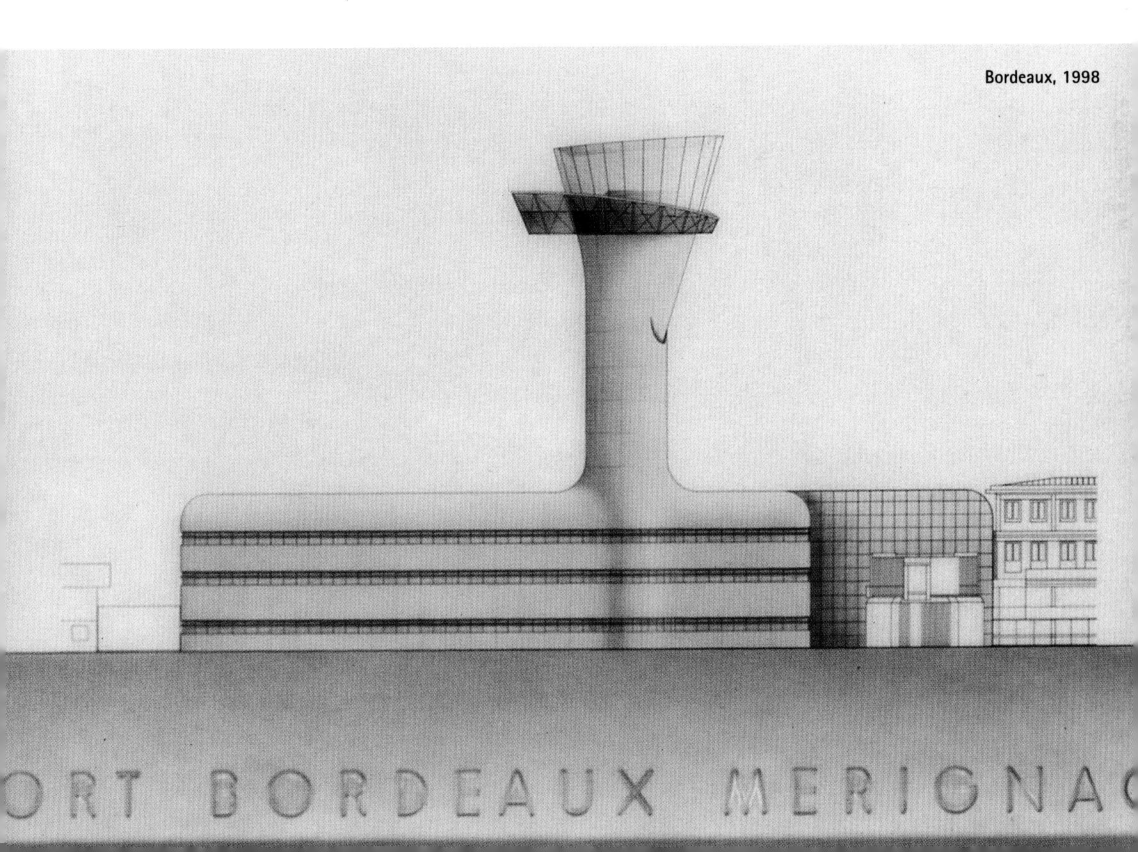

Bordeaux, 1998

packaging, clothes, toiletries, and cosmetics. There are precedents for some of these—the Saba jacket for Thomson, the Glacier bottled water package, the Fluocaril toothbrush, the Trois Suisses mail-order house. It seems like an enormous step forward, but it is also part of a slow progression, a further move in an approach to social design that has been discernible behind Starck's exuberant facade for years and is now being brought to the fore. The projects also illustrate how the strategy of the enemy within can operate to the advantage of all sides. La Redoute, for example, wanted a catalogue of Starck products, which they got, but with the addition of forty or so new products, exclusive to them, and presented in a wholly new way. In one sense the Good Goods catalogue could be said to be subverting the traditional approach of mail order, using the biggest mail-order company in Europe to do so. It is also creating choice, and specifically seeking to bring new customers to La Redoute. As for 7-11, "they asked me for the right to brand a couple of cheap product lines with my name," Starck explains, "and were a bit surprised to get back a proposal for forty or more products, all new and exclusive to them. Once they had got over the shock, they were delighted."

Others are still in shock, particularly after his new furniture designs, LWS and Neoz. "Some people in the furniture

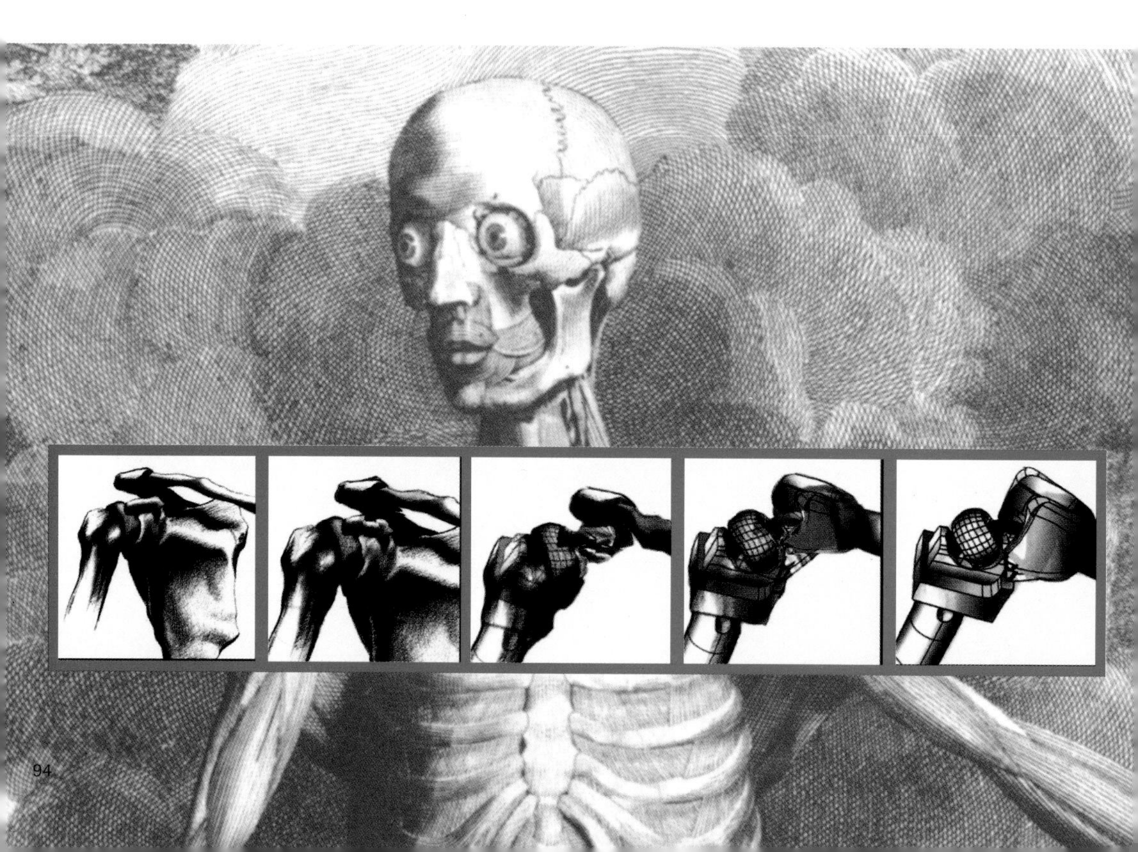

trade in France have been very dismissive of the Lazy Work Sofa, saying it has no design quality. These fools haven't just missed the point of the product, they are looking at the world the wrong way. The problem today is not 'What's the design content?' It is what is the social problem addressed, and what is the political solution found?" The excellent initial sales of the LWS line suggest that Starck, and not his critics in the furniture trade, has got the answer and the question right.

It is an old design adage, frequently cited but not often lived up to, that the best design work (in graphics, products, or interiors) should deliver more than the brief: not just what the client expects, but more than the client dreamed possible. This is a fair aim for any designer, but it only goes part of the way. The designer needs to remember that he or she has a responsibility not just to the client, but to a wider society at large, as well as a personal duty to maintain one's integrity. In other words, design is a political activity as much as a practical one. Thus, as Starck has pointed out, refusing to design may be the right answer. This is a deeply serious view of design: in my own view it is the only proper one. Starck has set himself the same goals of quality, decorating but not concealing them with wit, ambiguity, and humor.

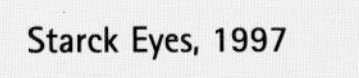

Starck Eyes, 1997

"If we want to bring about change," Starck says, "it's clear that the most important fundamental means for this is education. I'm not capable of being an educator; I haven't the patience or the training—or even much of an education myself. So once I realized that education was not a route open to me, I decided to make use of the subconscious, rather than the conscious. Because while the conscious speaks, it also tells lies. Often these lies don't matter, they're just about flattering the listener or the speaker, a set of convenient parameters around the subject. When the topic is unimportant, this lack of truth is unimportant, but when the subject is serious, a strategy of communicating with the subconscious is needed. One such strategy is to deal with actions that we make almost **without consciousness,** such as sleeping, eating, or going to the bathroom. As to the first, the starting point of my hotel designs is getting the pillows on the beds right. As to the last, I always said that when I had designed the perfect toilet brush I would give up design!"

Starck did design a toilet brush in 1994 (it is called, with his usual self-mockery, Excalibur), but he did not resign (so perhaps it is not perfect, though it is certainly fun). This approach is design from fundamentals, in all senses. It begins with modifying the semantic content of everyday images, for example by designing cars that do not shout speed,

Food

masculinity, and aggression, but speak of grace, comfort, and safety. Restaurants, bars, and hotels have always been part of his interior design and architectural practice, and he has designed kitchenware, chairs, and tables for several manufacturers. But in fall 1998 he took a completely new direction when he added food design to his repertoire.

For some years now Starck has been a vegetarian. This was a major conversion, as he says, "Like Buddha, I got to sanity after many stupidities! If now I'm someone who eats carefully and sensibly, it's because before I was the exact opposite. When I was eighteen I used to look out for tinned foods that had expanded under pressure, beans that fizzed like champagne. It amused me to eat rotted food. There was a certain game with death, a poetry of suicide in that. I was, for a long time, very suicidal, but now I'm an optimist, and a vegetarian." But not, being Starck, a conventional vegetarian. As he said at a conference in Barcelona in 1996, "When we eat meat, we kill. . . . Personally I don't give a damn about animals, the same way I don't give a damn about nature. But animals do suffer, and it bothers me to create angst." To the traditional dictum "we are what we eat," he now adds "we think how we eat. If we eat badly, we think badly, and live badly." He finds conventional vegetarian attitudes insufficient for three reasons: altruism, conservatism, and refusal.

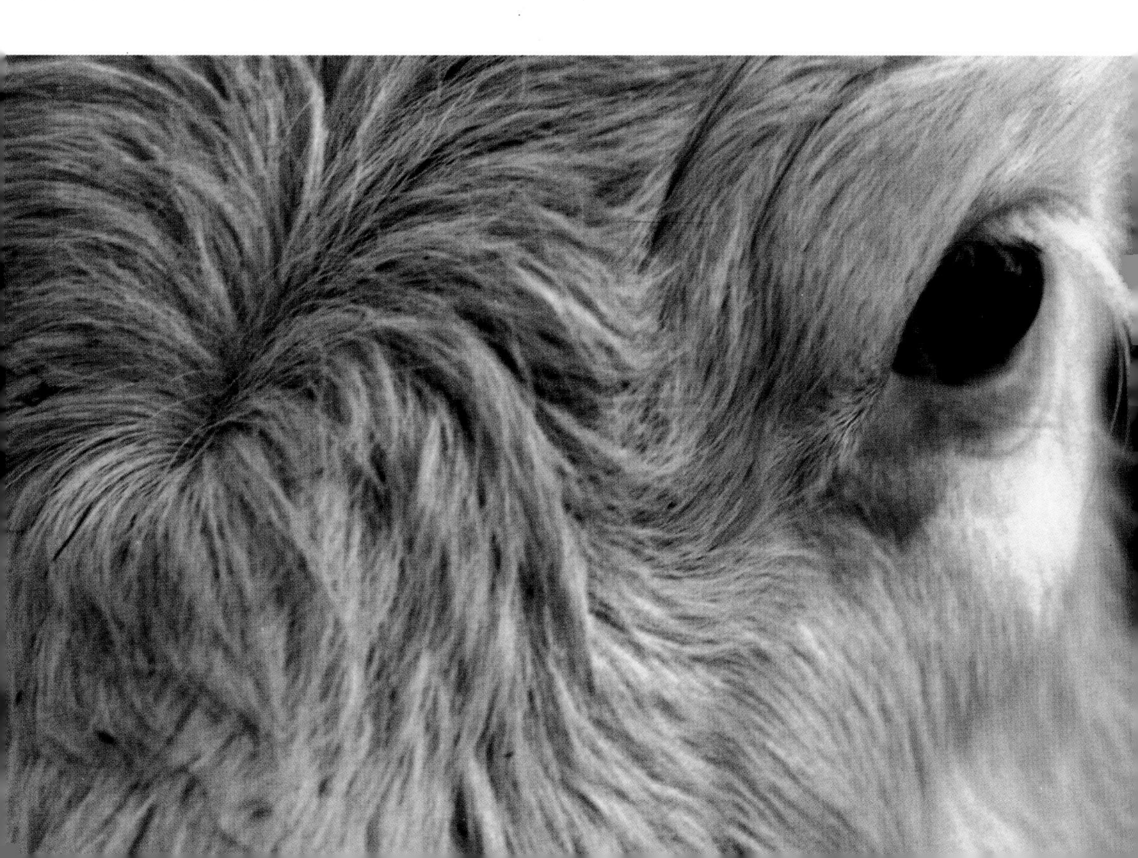

"My analysis begins with remembering that we are a mutant species, in mutation. Part of our species's romanticism is a sense of refusal, particularly a refusal to acknowledge our origins. It may be compensated for by an idea of progress, but we still overlook our **bestial origins.** And bestiality is defined by killing. So long as we continue to kill, we are tied to our origin among the beasts, however much we may deny it. Failing to recognize the link between killing and bestiality is to deny our origins, and so deny our own nature, our own existence, our own civilization. It is profoundly dishonest, it is not knowing who one is. Recognize the link, accept the necessity of mutation, and vegetarianism is the answer, because it breaks the chain that otherwise binds us to our origins. The philosophy of vegetarianism, if you like, can be seen as altruistic—at its most simple, I love my own children, so why eat some other creature's children? But altruism in not enough of a justification in itself, because of people's natural reticence—they don't want to make a great show of doing good, and so will refuse to for that reason. It's a reason I understand myself. I'm the most reticent person imaginable, always hiding my emotions. So the alternative tactic is to appeal to their personal interest: eat organically and you will feel better and live longer. That, they are able to accept, even if only out of egotism."

Conservatism looks only to the past, ignores the future, and so denies mutation. "I've never been interested in conservative people of any kind, they bore me," Starck explains. "I've long been a target for them, because I've always said that the new—even a mistake in bad taste—is always better than total intransigence to change, whether in good taste or not. Any new problem demands a new solution of the highest moral and creative order. I'm not interested in solutions based on old thinking and a denial of change." Abnegation, denial, and refusal (another aspect of classic vegetarianism—loving animals more than people) also mean opting out of society, denying one's humanity, an option to Starck that is equally if not more unacceptable.

After he had defined his personal position, there came the question of whether he could, as a designer, have an impact on the current **world of vegetarianism,** within his long-term strategic goals. His analysis suggested that even the best-marketed vegetarian products were reaching only those already converted. Having thought out an approach he went to see the directors of Lima, one of the oldest and largest European producers of vegetarian products; it was the only occasion in recent years that Starck went to the client. "I pointed out to them that their business was, structurally, marginal. They were selling only to those already convinced of the vegetarian argument. What if I can

recruit a new market for you? Say, among people of my age who, either because they want to improve their health or because they think it the right thing, as I do, want to become vegetarian but don't know how to, or among young people who live in front of the computer screen, joint in one hand, Coca-Cola in the other, never eating meat but who would never admit to being vegetarian as that was what their parents were back in the sixties. We can create products that those markets find accessible. Lima agreed. I have been working with them not just on the design of the packaging—the first time I've done any packaging design—but also on the composition and range of products, and the branding."

The initial launch includes forty-five products under the OAO logo. Prelaunch orders, which can be weak for a new food line, are excellent. I suspect that the key to the success of the OAO line lies in its linking the philosophical principles of vegetarianism and the health and societal issues of organic food to a **lifestyle approach.** For many, vegetarianism seems an ideological monolith, with a system of beliefs to be swallowed whole: you couldn't be a positive vegetarian three days a week, for example. The lifestyle approach makes it an option, and as such it is easier for the consumer to approach it and try it.

The product range was the first part of the strategy. The second part, again aimed at bringing outsiders into the organic fold, will be a series of restaurants, in the planning stage at the time this book was written. This is not a tactic of competition but of choice. "If you want to become even duller by eating dull neo-American food made from dead animals, you know where to go. But I'm making you an offer that is a parallel. The same basics, the same cost: all you get is more pleasure. The interior design will be full of delight and surprise, the staff will be prettier—or handsomer—because their health is better, the music will be better because it's intelligently chosen. It will all be more fun, and in addition, when you leave you'll feel better, you'll be in better health, you'll be more dynamic because you'll have shared the enthusiasm (strange how that word seems to be disappearing). And you will know why, because we will give you the information—not force it on you, but offer it freely—about how to eat intelligently, why amino acids are good for your brain, and so on."

Starck's reputation as a *bon viveur* was created in part by endless effusive articles describing the "wild boy" of French design with a bottle of champagne always open on the drawing board. One of the first OAO products is, in fact, a bottle of organic champagne, together with a selection of four organic wines. The champagne comes from the Fleury

vineyard, where Jean-Pierre Fleury and his colleagues have been practicing organic methods since 1992. But the list of OAO goods is not just framed by the selector's tastes. Wine is a symbol of companionship, of shared pleasures. Organic champagne is the deliberate antithesis of vegetarianism as refusal. It is also a reminder that organic methods of farming re-create tastes in foods that were lost with the introduction of mass-production agriculture. Where better to demonstrate this than through wine? As Starck says, "Quite apart from its more authentic taste, this champagne becomes the prototype for new relationships between people, the production system, the environment, and themselves."

Other products in the OAO line include olive oil and vinegar, couscous, noodles, rice cakes, oat milk, and three pâtés. The OAO logo is discrete: a simple set of sans serif capitals, either printed grey on white or embossed onto the packaging itself. The choice of packing solutions is innovative: sealed foil and paper Tetrapaks for the oat milk, for example, and a cleverly engineered system for instant foods in which the folded paper container holds the food after hot water has been added. For the basic foodstuffs such as rice and spaghetti, the pack is deliberately perforated with cellophane inserts to show the product within. As to the product graphics, the associated colors are grays or dark

greens, with an orange panel for nutritional information. The panel also serves as a link between the product and the consumer, explaining and encouraging the organic approach to food.

Though the fidelity of the individual foods to organic and vegetarian principles is not compromised, the OAO range is not a complete dietary solution, nor is it intended to be. The OAO line is about options: the consumer can use it as the foundation of a dedicated organic and vegetarian diet or as part of a plan for healthier eating. As Starck puts it, "When it comes to fighting, I'm not a boxer; I practice *aikido*. I'm not interested in direct combat: it's tiring, it's dangerous, it's expensive, it's out-of-date. I prefer to set up a counterweight, against which the opposition falls from its own efforts." The counterweight is the argument in favor of the organic and vegetarian approach to food. In its own terms, it is unassailable: no one can justify eating in an unhealthy way. Starck leaves the choice to the consumer. "Liberty is the necessary style of the future," Starck explains, "so I am not trying to dictate taste or choice. We are all different from each other, and within ourselves we are different from moment to moment and from time to time. I am suggesting options for those moments of difference, saying 'you can,' not 'you must'—the difference between a conservative or ideological approach, which denies the individual, and a contemporary approach, which values the individual."

CHAMPAGNE
Jean-Pierre Fleury
Sélectionné par OAO
BRUT
75cl
12%vol
Contrôle Ecocert

This is all quite simple, Starck explains: "nonobjects for nonconsumers in the future moral market." Some time ago Starck was approached by the largest mail-order business in Europe, La Redoute, which wanted to produce a special catalogue containing only Philippe Starck products. Starck had already worked with mail order for his Trois Suisses house and other designs and understood the reach of such media, especially in France: "As large as television, but lasts longer," as he once put it. For La Redoute he amassed a collection of products to be sold through the Good Goods catalogue. Some are his own work, some created by others and endorsed by Starck. The products were selected not for their style, but for their functionality and anonymity: Good Goods is a workmanlike grouping. They are nonproducts in that they deal with basic necessities (clothing, cookware, lighting, seating, etc.) rather than luxury.

By "nonconsumers," Starck explains that he means those who feel marginalized by the current consumerism of society but who need, like everyone else, to dress, to eat, to sleep, and so need the appurtenances of modern life—those he hopes to interest in the new catalogue. Starck feels that the position of the nonconsumer, though admirable in some respects, is at heart a refusal, and so inevitably disengages the nonconsumer from society as a whole, not just from those aspects he or she does not like. If society is to develop—or mutate—away from consuming toward

caring, it is precisely the involvement of such people that society needs, and in offering them a series of products Starck is offering them a channel for a positive statement about society. In short, Starck's aim is to politicize these social dissenters.

Mail order as a popular method of purchasing has developed in France in the twentieth century for much the same reasons it developed in the United States in the nineteenth: geographical distances (though on a smaller scale). Mail-order services developed, particularly after World War II, as a means of bringing urban consumer choices to those outside urban areas. French mail-order catalogues offer a full range of major, branded consumer kitchen appliances, consumer electronics and kitchenware, and fashion, as well as the company's own products, similar to the old Sears, Roebuck catalogue. Starck, using the "enemy within" approach, sets out an alternative. "I wanted to use the skills and the tools of this system to offer a **different definition** of the consumer," he explains, "and La Redoute, from the president downward, has accepted this opportunity, this challenge." The value to him of the mail-order approach is that it keeps the products out of the normal retail chain, and so offers a direct route to the consumer. It also allows the products to be presented on their own, in a context in which the reasoning behind the choice can be explained,

and literally be read by the consumer, if he or she wishes, at leisure. This is in complete contrast to the pressurized atmosphere of a retail shop or shopping mall. It is both an extension and a subversion of the mail-order concept. Thus each product in the resulting La Redoute/Good Goods catalogue comes with an explanatory notice, a method also used in the catalogue. "Normally the consumer makes choices based on immediate perceptions—'I like this' or 'I don't want that'—while here there is an explanation of the value of the product, within this new definition of the consumer in a moral market, and, by implication, a criticism of the failings of other products, designed for the consuming consumer," according to Starck, "so even if the consumer decides not to buy, he or she is making an informed decision." Herein lies the definition of the future moral marketplace, one in which consumer decisions are not driven by subjective criteria. In the moral market the consumer makes positive, objective (including the decision to say no) decisions based on his or her own values.

For Starck, the moral market is not an abstract. "I'm a designer—if you like, a designer of Christmas presents! I can talk about the moral market and write about the moral market, but my only way of honestly engaging with it is to be designing for it. Because then I am not only saying to the consumer, 'You should buy this kind of product,' I'm also

saying, 'Here is the actual product: buy it and try it.' The element of verification of the offer is important. This is, I accept, a risky process for me. I'm putting my reputation behind the products I endorse. But I think any designer has to have both that kind of honesty and the will to push his or her own potential to its limits. And that same honesty and effort should induce the same honesty in the consumer, who is faced not with an abstract concept, but with a real decision: to buy or not to buy, or at least to accept or not the arguments for a moral market. In this way Good Goods is also a political tool, popular and subversive, which goes to the heart of the process of consumption."

The Good Goods catalogue is a mixture of existing pure Starck products, existing products branded by Starck, new Starck products, and products endorsed by Starck from other designers. Its aim is to furnish the needs of the ideal future consumer—the balanced, involved, aware, caring citizen of tomorrow. The initial plan was for a catalogue of two hundred items, of which one hundred and forty would be "by Starck" in some way. Starck himself realizes the hubris of this situation, but as he says, "First, La Redoute wanted a catalogue 'signed by Starck': they were not initially interested in the wider proposal. Second, if each product is to be accompanied by a critical text, I prefer to be seen criticizing my own products."

TOMORROW WILL BE LESS

"Starck Hits Fashion" must have been a dream headline for many a lifestyle editor in a dull month. Now it's happened, but not as they may have dreamed. Not the collection signed Gaultier/Starck or even a range fronting new, young designers. Instead, a collection with K-Way, first-class producers of reliable all-weather clothes, and the NC collection, meaning No Creation, No Chemicals: basics like pullovers, shirts, and socks, and clothes for babies. And a simple, bias-cut adjustable-length woman's dress, for Wolford. But if the fashion editors of the world will not be pleased, they are not those whom Starck was setting out to please.

One important element in the clothing section is the T-shirt. The T-shirt is such a ubiquitous accessory that we forget that it is quite recent: the liberating American armies introduced it to Europe (the liberated Europeans were hardly likely to take the British Army's vests as a symbol of freedom) and Hollywood promoted it on James Dean and Marlon Brando. It became the world's first unisex garment, and then a platform for slogans, brand loyalties, and modern tribal identifications with rock groups, sports teams, and fashion names. In the two collections of T-shirts Starck has included in Good Goods, one of these principles is ignored and the other subverted. The first collection, called 'Nine Months,' comprises a set of women's T-shirts, designed by Patricia Baile, for wear during pregnancy. They have

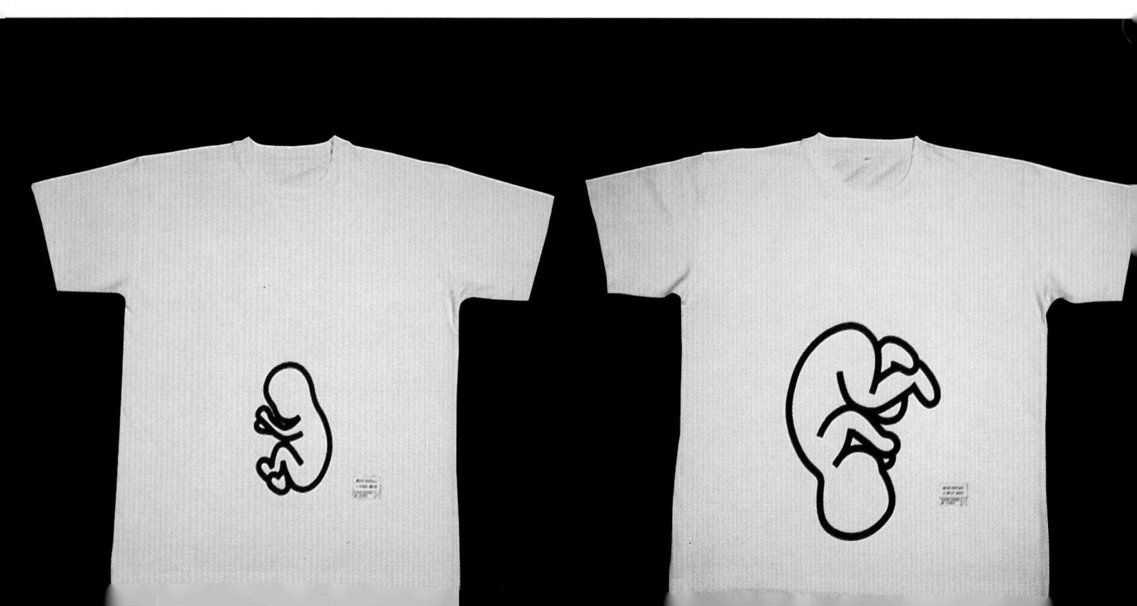

therefore been designed and cut to widen progressively around the waistline to accommodate the growing child, and each month's shirt is decorated with a changing image of a fetus in development. No longer the unisex ubiquitous fashion item, these T-shirts become a way of marking, practically, a basic, loving, and important human process.

The second series (which is unisex) carries basic slogans, devised by Starck, set in simple sans serif capital type, without any logo or decoration. The slogans are familiar to anyone who has followed Starck's recent thinking, but the absence of logo or signature invites the wearer to identify with the proposal, not with the designer. It brings the nonconsumers out into the open and invites them to signal their position with a nonbranded statement. Statements such as "Tomorrow will be less," "God is dangerous," "Moral Market," "Le civisme est d'avant-garde" (Civil society is the way forward), or "Nous sommes des mutants" (We are all mutants) are expressed directly and plainly for the wearer to adopt. This contradicts the usual approach of the T-shirt, which by carrying the name of a designer or the logo of a trendy manufacturer invites the wearer to make a statement about belonging to a consuming group, not an independent statement for him or herself. And the modern T-shirt is, in a sense, duplicitous, in that the wearer

buys the right to wear the brand or the name, but there is no reciprocity involved: you acknowledge the brand, but the brand does not recognize you. This itself is contrary to an earlier tradition of branded clothing; for example, Scottish tartans, which were the visible signals of a system of interrelated obligations and kinships.

Where is the interest in designing inexpensive products? The financial return is minimal and the cost/quality restraints are very tight. The Good Goods catalogue is a mixture of existing products by Starck and other designers, and new projects by Starck himself, often in collaboration with established manufacturers either in the ecological sector or in the design sector. Among the existing products are such Starck chairs as Dr. No, Lord Yo, Miss Tripp, and Prince Aha. Add to these the new series of Cheap Chic chairs (a standard frame with molded polyurethane backs in five different colors.) There is also the new La Marie chair, made in rigid polyurethane, transparent or with a translucent color tint. Starck describes it as the ultimate minimal chair, almost the final definition of **the nonproduct.** It is deliberately inexpensive. Other furniture includes Citterio's Mobil modular storage system. The lighting section has work by Starck, including the new Archimoon series, as well as lamps by Droog Design, Ingo Maurer, and Konstantin Grcic.

JE SUIS SEREIN
I AM CALM
JE VOIS L'INVISIBLE
I SEE THE INVISIBLE
JE SUIS CURIEUSE
I AM CURIOUS
JE CONSOMME PEU
I USE SPARINGLY
JE SUIS SAGE
I AM WISE
WITH
LA REDOUTE

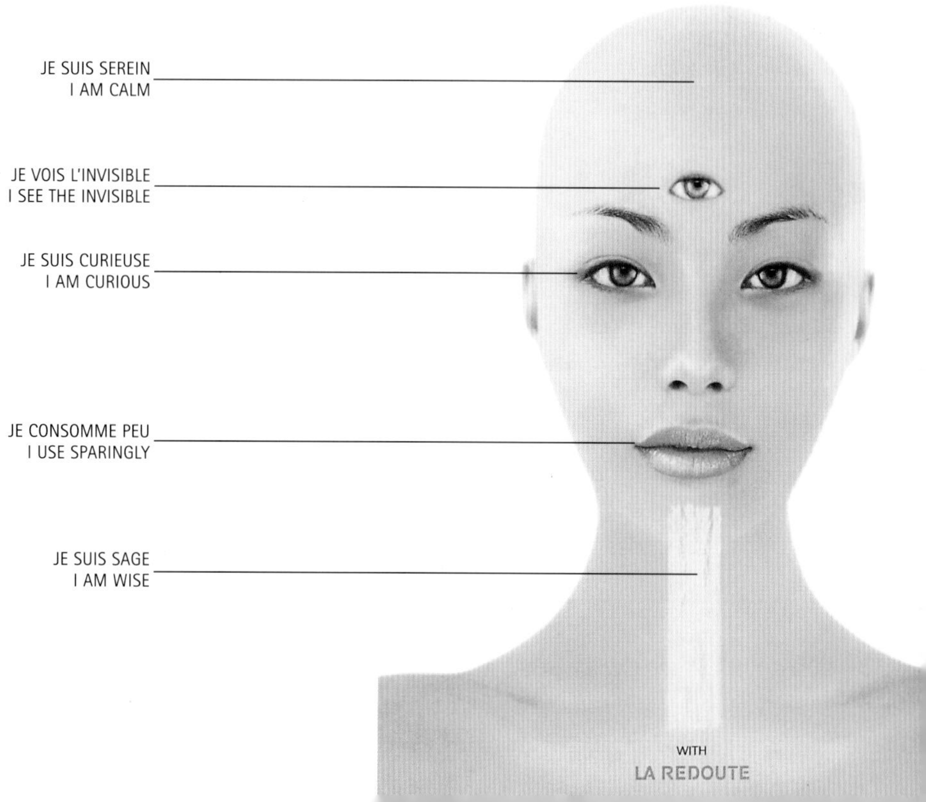

In the housewares section Starck's own Dr. Skud flyswatter for Alessi is complemented by the Boaat series of food containers, also from Alessi, by Droog Design's Salad Sunrise oil and vinegar bottle, and for home entertainment, the Alessi/Thomson range, including Moosk, Ola, Don-O, and Pala Pala. A selection of music CDs from Virgin in metal cases, special editions of books from Le Serpent a Plumes, sunglasses by Mikli, a scooter, a bicycle, and a kayak, and interactive children's games are also included. There are the OAO range of organic foods, body-care products from Bioderma, soaps from green product specialists Ecover.

Another section is for protective equipment—dust and smog masks, smoke detectors, and life jackets. The disturbing presence of these items is a reminder of the serious purpose behind the project, that the moral market exists in a society *in* danger and replete *with* dangers. Good Goods is not just about celebrating the good things in life, but about real issues as well.

Good Goods is the culmination of a process of reflection on Starck's part that began with the idea of a "Company Without Death," an extension of his vegetarian principles, through a "Good Food" concept—which became OAO—into the complete, caring, and human proposal that is Good Goods.

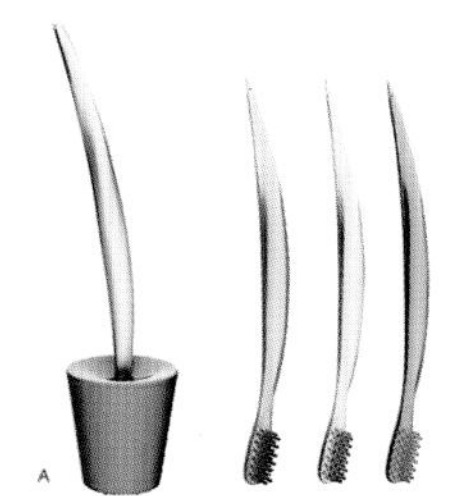

A

ss. Sorte de végétal cristallisé, Dr Kiss devient une petite sculpture ans la salle de bains. Objet simple d'emploi quotidien, cette brosse de mes fiertés, créée dans le bonheur avec mon ami, Alberto Alessi. s a colourful sculpture, a delightful presence in your bathroom. A oject for daily use, this toothbrush, which I designed happily with Alberto Alessi, is a pride to me.
Philippe Starck, **éditeur**: Alessi, **produit**: Dr Kiss, **date de on**: 1997, **date de production**: 1998, **description**: brosse à dents e conique en ABS (diamètre 5cm, hauteur 5,5cm), hauteur totale **férences**: orange 700.8180, rose 701.2152, violet 701.2187, jaune , **prix**: 100 F/15,08 Euros. Lot 4 brosses à dents sans la base, **es**: orange 572.1105, rose 572.1130, violet 572.1148, jaune , **prix**: 120 F/18,09 Euros, **en 24h chez vous**: +80F/12,06 Euros.

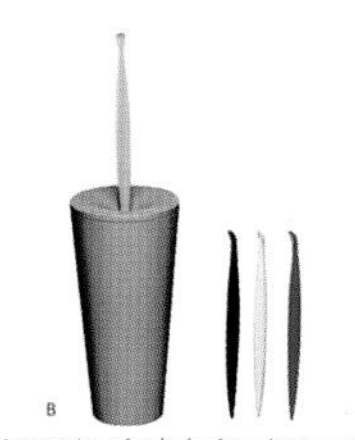

B

B. Dr Spoon. Le coton-tige, même le plus doux, n'est pas un véritable ami des oreilles. Un objet d'origine asiatique, la cuiller à oreilles, nous apprend l'utilité de revisiter une procédure ancestrale. Dr Spoon prouve qu'il est évidemment plus juste d'extraire avec précaution le cérumen.
Dr Spoon. The cotton swab, no matter how soft, is no friend of the ear. Of Asian origin, the ear spatula shows us that we have much to learn from reviewing ancestral procedures. Dr Spoon proves that it is much more sensible to gently remove earwax.
Design: Philippe Starck, **éditeur**: Alessi, **produit**: Dr Spoon, **date de conception**: 1997, **date de production**: 1998, **description**: lot de 4 petites spatules cure-oreilles en résine thermoplastique avec base en ABS, base diamètre 4,5cm, hauteur 9cm, spatule 8,3cm, finition satinée, **référence**: 530.6531 (produit disponible à partir de mi-octobre 1998), **prix**: 110 F/16,59 Euros, **en 24h chez vous**: +80F/12,06 Euros.

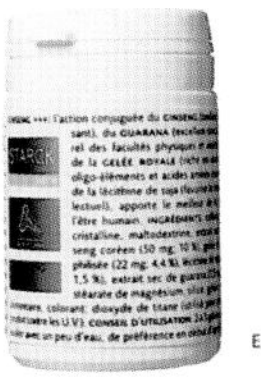

E

E. Ginseng+++ Starck with Europ-Labo. Complexe fortifiant, dynamisant et stimulant général de l'organisme, tant sur un plan physique que psychique. Un concentré de substances naturellement prodigieuses: ginseng, guarana, gelée royale et lécithine de soja.
Starck with Europ-Labo ginseng+++. A complex which fortifies, energizes, and stimulates the organism, on both a psychic and physical level. It is a concentration of naturally powerful substances: ginseng, guarana, royal jelly, lecithin.
Produit: Ginseng+++ Starck with Europ-Labo, **contenance**: 55 gélules, **référence**: 701.6140, **prix**: 95 F/14,32 Euros, **en 24h chez vous**: +80F/12,06 Euros.

F

F. Gélules de propolis Starck with Europ-Labo. Tonique général et revitalisant. Riche en flavonoïdes, en essences et en acides naturels, elle est un remarquable soutien pour stimuler les défenses naturelles, lutter efficacement contre les agressions extérieures et favoriser la résistance cellulaire et la vitalité de l'organisme.
Starck with Europ-Labo propolis capsules. Propolis, a general revitalizing tonic, rich in bioflavinoids, essences, and natural acids. Propolis boosts the body's resistance to disease, arms it against outside agression, and promotes the organism's vitality and cellular resilience.
Produit: Gélules de propolis Starck with Europ-Labo, **contenance**: 75 gélules, **référence**: 705.4980, **prix**: 65 F/9,80 Euros, **en 24h chez vous**: +80F/12,06 Euros.

G

G. Gelée royale fraîche Starck with Europ Labo. Reconstituant et stimulant, renforce le défenses naturelles de l'organisme. Elle concentre des éléments vitaux et convient pour tous Particulièrement recommandée aux jeunes e périodes de croissance, aux convalescents, au personnes âgées, aux personnes fatiguées stressées, déprimées.
Starck with Europ-Labo fresh royal jelly. tonic and stimulant, it reinforces the body's natural defenses. This concentrate of vital elements i beneficial to people of all ages, but it is especially recommended for young people durin growth spurts, convalescents, elderly people and anyone who feels tired, depressed, or subject to stress.
Produit: Gelée royale fraîche Starck with Europ Labo, **contenance**: 65 capsules, **référence** 704.4496, **prix**: 95 F/14,32 Euros, **en 24h che vous**: +80F/12,06 Euros.

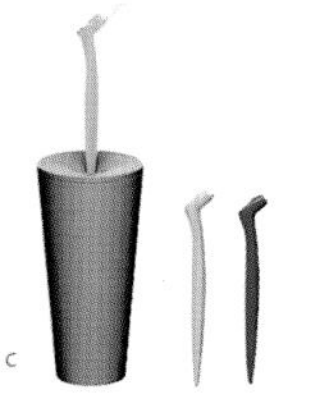

C

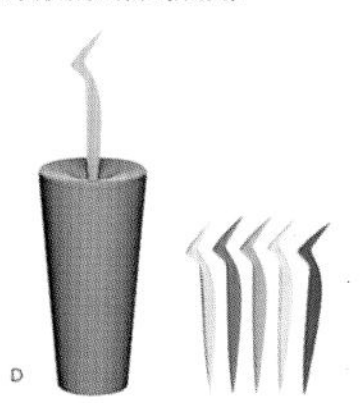

D

eese. La brosse interdentaire évite l'installation des microbes, la formation de la plaque dentaire, et, par extension, prévient le déchaussement des dents. e en 3mn, l'opération de nettoyage avec la brossette devient aussi normale qu'un brossage classique et procure un sentiment de véritable bien-être.
se. The interdental brush prevents bacteria from settling in the spaces between the teeth and forming plaque which causes gums to recede. The nute cleaning you accomplish with the interdental brush soon becomes as normal as conventional brushing, and provides a feeling of true well-being.
Philippe Starck, **éditeur**: Alessi, **produit**: Dr Cheese, **date de conception**: 1997, **date de production**: 1998, **description**: brosse interdentaire en ermoplastique livrée avec 6 brossettes interchangeables, base conique en ABS (diamètre 4,5cm, hauteur 9cm), manche hauteur 8cm, finition **éférence**: jaune, 530.6779, bleu 633.0380, **prix**: 130 F/19,60 Euros. Lot 6 brossettes (non photographié), **référence**: 572.1008, **prix**: 35 F/5,28 **24h chez vous**: +80 F/12,06 Euros (tous ces produits disponibles à partir de mi-octobre 1998).
een. Ce cure-dents en matière de synthèse est amical pour les gencives. On peut le conserver dans une salle de bains sur son socle, mais c'est n instrument de sauvetage à emmener avec soi.
. This synthetic toothpick is kind to your mouth. Dr Kleen can remain on its stand, near the bathroom sink, but it is especially an excellent travel-panion, apt to provide succor when the need arises.
Philippe Starck, **éditeur**: Alessi, **produit**: Dr Kleen, **date de conception**: 1994, **date de production**: 1998, **description**: Lot de 6 cure-dents mide, base conique en ABS (diamètre 4,5cm, hauteur 9cm), cure-dents 7,7cm, **référence**: 701.5453, **prix**: 100 F/15,08 Euros. **hez vous**: +80 F/12,06 Euros.

H

H. Gel d'aloès Starck with Europ-Labo. Gel hydratant*. L'aloe vera, ou aloès, est une plante grasse des régions chaudes et arides qui renferme dans se feuilles un suc amer utilisé depuis l'Antiquité pour ses vertus médicinales. Gel cosmétique qui convient à toutes les peaux, particulièrement recommand en cas de fragilité cutanée, en cas d'irritations, de piqûres d'insectes, d'exposition au soleil. Il aide la peau à retrouver élasticité et souplesse en laissant un sensation de fraîcheur. Propriétés apaisantes et cicatrisantes. Bénéfique après le rasage. *Hydratation des couches supérieures de l'épiderme.
Starck with Europ-Labo aloe vera gel. A moisturizing gel*. Aloe Vera is a succulent plant which grows in hot, arid regions. Its leaves contain a bitter juic which has been used for medicinal purposes since Antiquity. This gel treatment is suitable for all skin types, and is especially recommended for the relief skin irritation due to chapping, insect bites, sunburn, or windburn. It restores the skin's elasticity and softness leaving a refreshing feeling. Healing, soothin properties. A good after-shave treatment. *Moisturization of the skin's outer layer.
Produit: Gel d'aloès Starck with Europ-Labo, **contenance**: 50ml, **référence**: 739.5205, **prix**: 45 F/6,79 Euros (prix au décilitre: 90F/dl), **en 24h chez vous** +80F/12,06 Euros.

In his campaign to reach wide, general markets, Starck must have been delighted to get a call from the 7-11 chain of convenience stores in Japan. The franchise has 14,000 stores throughout Southeast Asia, of which over 3,500 are in Japan. Like their Western counterparts, they are small stores selling basic goods, and open twenty-four hours a day, seven days a week. In addition to basic foodstuffs (including instant noodles, soups, and teas sold hot), they sell a basic range of toiletries, office staples, and basic kitchenwares such as napkins, chopsticks, and plastic cups. The shops in Japan also function as village stores and post offices: you can pay taxes and utility bills there, use free phones for booking travel, and send baggage to airports. They are also Japan's local newsstands and tobacconists. They can be found not only in urban areas, but also in the countryside.

In the particular rituals of Japanese life they are largely masculine haunts, especially in the late evening after the bars close. Salarymen on the way home stop for a snack or a coffee, or to stock up on necessities. According to Starck, they are also frequented by cyberjunkies, whose clocks are determined by download times not solar movements. This group of social marginals interested Starck, as they are nonconsumers par excellence.

To meet the demand for Western goods so prevalent in Japan—even in the basic ranges of goods offered by 7-11—

7-11

the company had invited famous designers and fashion names to label particular products, often manufactured in South China or Taiwan, in a simple and direct royalty operation. Starck saw in the invitation wider possibilities: not single products but product lines, and not labeling but the creation of real, inexpensive products exclusive to 7-11. The first two series of goods are office and bathroom basics. (A series of kitchenware basics such as chopsticks and bottle openers is in preparation; eventually the Starck range will cover almost all the goods in the store.) The office range includes pencils and ballpoint pens, scissors, tape dispensers, and staplers. They are presented in uniform silver boxes, with a brick-red interior and a clear cellophane front bearing the message "Tomorrow will be less" printed in red. The bathroom range includes toothbrushes and hairbrushes, an FM radio, cotton balls, and scissors. These are presented in a silver plastic base carrying the Starck logo, with a rectangular transparent cellophane box above. The packaging sizes match 7-11's shelving system: they are **deliberately anonymous,** as befits containers for basic goods. The bathroom products have an additional feature: a slot under the base fits into a tray, also designed by Starck, that holds a row of several items. The user can keep and use the packaging as a bathroom fixture. For the cotton swabs, the slot is open, so that the products can be removed from it singly, from beneath, even when in the tray.

"Because my name is well known in Japan," Starck explains, "7-11 asked me to badge some products for them. I replied with a proposal for a whole range of products. I think they were a bit surprised! Are you serious? So I sent a second set of further proposals. They said yes. It is the same kind of subversive, guerrilla strategy I have used elsewhere. I'm in the fortunate position of receiving far more offers than I can accept, so I only choose those projects that lead to a situation where people will be better, in terms of being citizens of a new society. And as a guerrilla tactic, it is a fair one: the consumers get better goods, created with more intelligence and love, the manufacturers make a profit, and I spread my message more widely, in this case to a new group." The nondesign proposal succeeds, ironically enough, because it has the authority of a designer behind it. It is interesting to compare this to another Japanese chain, Muji, which has earned in the West something of a cult status for its product lines (office and kitchen equipment, toiletries, and clothes) precisely because it is a "no-name" brand. Mikli uses flat shades of gray, or white and black, on simple undecorated shapes. Their very anonymity makes them identifiable, and thus a fashion statement rather than a necessity.

The 7-11 project also represents a continuing interest in the modern Japanese way of life, particularly of the male

office workers who form a key part of the chain's clientele in the evenings. The often anonymous lifestyle of the *chonga* (Japanese slang for bachelor) led Starck in 1990 to the Moondog project. The project is for a block of one-room bachelor apartments, set on ziggurats and surmounted by a conical building that resembles a rocket or shell, which would house a restaurant, a bar, and other communal facilities.

As Starck explained in a 1997 lecture, "In Tokyo houses have numbers, but the numbers are not in order. So I thought of the bachelors, working in an anonymous office all day and returning to an anonymous room in an anonymous house every night, and designed Moondog. **'Where do you live?'** an acquaintance would ask. 'In the rocket ship over there' would be the reply." At first glance, and without knowing its purpose, the design (which was never built) looks somewhat threatening, despite its cartoon coloring and the blue-and-white checkerboard pattern on the sides. Once its purpose is understood, it becomes a benign and fun rocket to the moon, not a war machine. If Moondog offers a light-hearted but serious approach to a social problem, by making the anonymous home an identifiable landmark, so the 7-11 range turns anonymous products into real ones, made for a specific market. They are not offered with a fashion signature draped across the front, but with a designer's thought behind them.

At the 1998 Cologne Industrial Fair the lighting designer Ingo Maurer had a party. On arrival, each guest was presented with a cardboard mask printed with Starck's features, which they were invited to wear for the evening, while admiring Maurer's new and very phallic design, called Horny Philippe. Inside, the mask bore the motto "De la technologie à l'amour: or the Transfiguration of Horny Philippe." "From Technology to Love" was a subtle and witty designer to another: the French phrase is Starck's own, used to describe his work for Thomson. It also acknowledged the change that has become apparent in Starck's approach to design in the last few years, though, as we have seen, the roots of that change are deep.

At present Starck is attempting to politicize his activity as a designer, identifying himself, his design, and his philosophy with a part of the market he perceives to be rebelling against a consuming society. It is a bold proposal, given the range of products it covers. In two areas, food and fashion, he has no track record (apart from a design for bottled water for Glacier and the Saba jacket for Thomson). He assumes that the strength of his reputation will enable him to convey his message to willing listeners. What are the precedents for such a design gesture? Should it, and will it, succeed?

Tomo

One major precedent for politically motivated design lies in the efforts made in the early years of the Soviet Union to reshape the material world in Communist terms. As the textile designer Varvara Stepanova wrote in the magazine *Lef* in 1923, "Fashion which psychologically reflects the '*byt,*' that is, custom and aesthetic taste, is giving way to programmed clothing, produced in order to suit the work which the wearer is carrying out in different sectors or for a precise social action. . . . It is not enough to provide intelligent designs. They need to be made on the production line and given a practical demonstration at work; only then will it be possible to have a clear image of them. . . . Today's clothing must be seen 'in action,' outside of this it is unimaginable, just as any machine is absurd outside of its own work. All decorative detail is abolished with the following slogan: 'The comfort and practicality of clothing must be linked to a specific practical function.' Not only is mass control on what clothes are worn necessary but clothing must also pass on from being the product of an artisan to that of industrial mass production. Thus clothing loses its 'ideological' meaning and becomes an aspect of cultural reality."

In addition to design driven by purely political ends, there are **models of design** that saw opportunities in political constraints. One such model is the DIN, the system of industrial regulation introduced by the German government

rrow

during World War I, initially as a quality-control mechanism for armament production, and later covering all kinds of standards and measures. The A4, A3, A2, A1 paper system used widely in Europe, for example, was created by the DIN as a way of printing as economically as possible from a one-meter-square sheet of paper. A broader and later example is the Utility clothing and furniture program that began in Britain during World War II. Gordon Russell, a furniture maker and member of the advisory panel on Utility furniture, wrote at the time, "the interesting feature of the scheme is that there has been a definite and conscious effort to grade up both design and specification. Through it the public has become accustomed to a much better and simpler type of design."

None of these three approaches is an entirely appropriate model today: for all its initial optimism, the idea of clothing the proletariat as a way of fashioning his thinking became a grim and cynical farce. The German approach, based on the Taylorisms of heavy industry, is efficient but soulless, and finds its echo in the "black is best" look created by Dieter Rams for Braun, or in the drab gray that is the hallmark of computer manufacturers. And if Utility furniture is a rare collector's item today, it is because the ordinary people of Britain replaced it with something they liked more. The Utility approach is simply to patronize the client, not to offer choice or information.

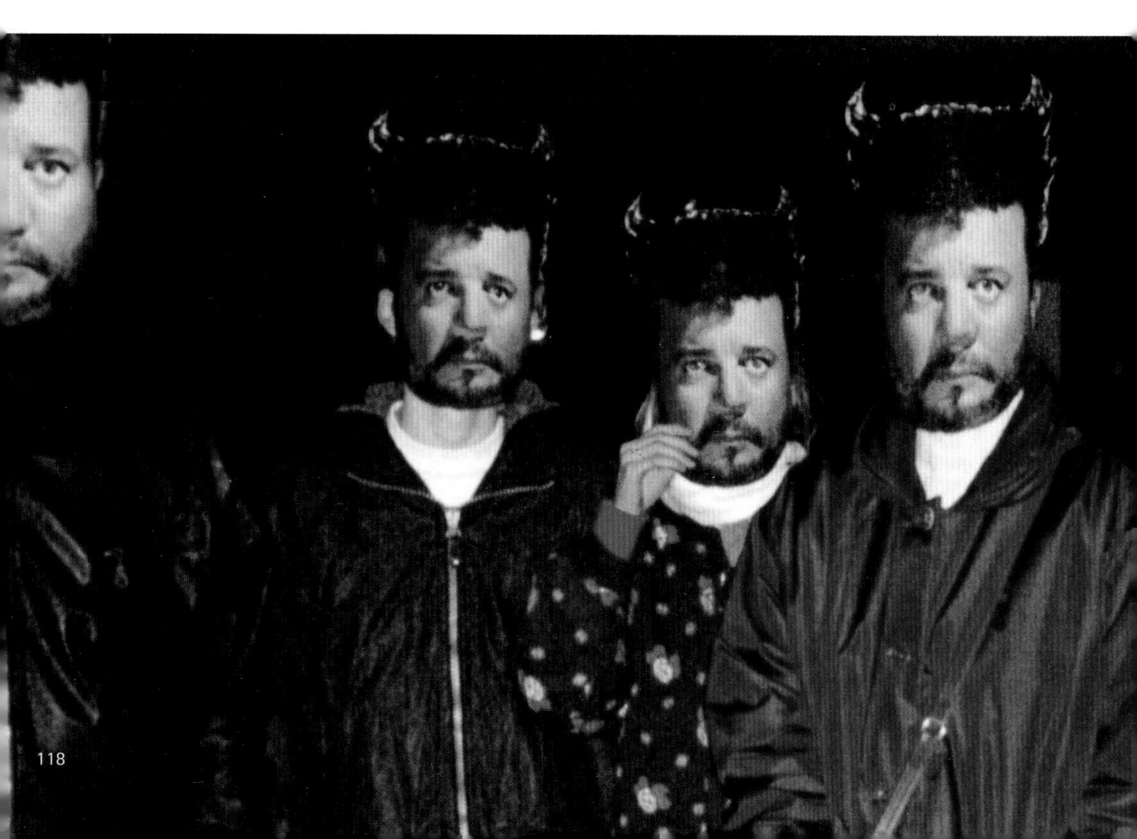

More recently, individual designers and groups have sought to turn design to specific social and political ends. For example, Jane Atfield in England uses recycled plastics for her furniture and lighting. This work is both interesting and fun, but it is essentially part of a dialogue within the design community.

"All my work for the last two, two and a half years," Starck explained to me in early 1998, "has been to create a political movement—not a political party as such—but to use my skill and knowledge as a designer to address a particular social group, the nonconsumers. They are rebels, they are suspicious of society. What I am trying to do is wake them up, to make them consciously aware of their unconscious position, and to give them the tools to recognize themselves and each other so that, by joining together, their views can have an effect. The nonconsumer today has the potential, which the Greens and ecologists had and lost, of being the new left. But too often the ecologists were innate conservatives. I see the awakened nonconsumer as an active rebel, no longer a passive one, no longer a spectator but an actor. This is a militant position on my part, designed to provoke a reaction. There are those who are against progress, or outside society. Fine—that's their choice. But my choice is to act. We are mutants in a mutating society. Finding the right solutions to the actual situation is a challenge and a duty."

Starck Now

The year 1998 was a major one for Starck. During it more than three hundred new products saw the light of day, and a raft of new projects were started or developed. The range of products gives visual form to the evolution of his design strategy, already discussed, toward a radicalization and politicization of his position. Over the next forty or so pages we present a selection from this astonishing output, including the Good Goods work for La Redoute, the OAO food range, and furniture designs for Driade and Cassina. **122** TeddyBearBand children's toy from Good Goods: in Starck's words "a single toy that would serve as an apprenticeship for the lasting human relationships that await our children." **123** Starck as Shiva (the products are prototype shoe, Eau St. Georges, Excalibur, Dede, TooYoo, and Miss Sissi). **125** Kayak Starck by Rotomod. **126** Wet Duke waterproof jacket designed by Starck for K-Way: the collection is called Wet Elegance, and according to Starck is intended "to make available completely functional clothing that takes its cue from an urban, modern concept of elegance." **127** Wet Prince, by Starck for K-Way. **128/9** Starck Naked, a one-piece variable dress/skirt designed by Starck for Wolford: "the missing link in women's wear: of minimal weight and bulk, maximum flexibility, and truly multipurpose application." **130/1** Eyeglass frames for Mikli, by Starck: "the nonproduct of the future: technologically advanced, emancipative, and guided by a quest for the minimum." **132** Cheap Chic chairs by Starck for XO in 1997, stacking aluminum-framed chairs with tinted polypropylene seats: "part of a quest for borderline anonymity." **133** La Marie chair in transparent or opaque polycarbonate, designed for Kartell in 1998: "perhaps my ultimate chair. Archetypal, humble, and selfless." **134/5** The Archizoom lamp uses a standard base with different reflectors (Soft, Tech, Eco, and Classic) for different tasks: produced by Flos, 1998. The Archimoon Soft (page 135) is "an architect's light with a distinctly human feel." **136** The Boaat range of food storage dishes, designed by Starck for Alessi, 1998. **137** Dr. Skud, a flyswatter in tinted polycarbonate, by Starck for Alessi, 1998. Other Alessi products in the catalogue include the Moosk radio (designed by Gérôme Olivet), the Coo-Coo clock-radio and Faitoo cutlery, by Starck. **138/9** Four music CDs, created by Starck with Virgin. Starck selected the music on each, according to the themes of heart, body, head, and conscience: "above all, I love sound, regardless of its cultural or epochal source." **140** Author Joao Ubaldo Ribeiro photographed by D. Moldzinski. **141** *Afrique*, one of four collections of stories ("four anthologies of fiction from five continents") published by Le Serpent à Plumes in a package designed by Starck. **142/5** The Aprilia 6.5 motorbike designed by Starck is in the catalogue, as is a standard bike with electric engine, the Peugeot Vélectron, and a push-scooter by Bauwerk (products not designed by Starck). **146/7** Tablets for dishwashers, fabric conditioners, and washing liquid created by Ecover and packaged by Starck for Good Goods. Each package has a descriptive label explaining the ecological value of the contents. Other ecological products badged by Starck include Bioderma cosmetics, Biofa paints, and food supplements from Europ-Labo. **148/9** Two organic olive oils from the OAO range from Lima (the OAO products are also offered in the Good Goods catalogue). "You will find," Starck says, "that organic foods are not only healthier, they are tastier as well. OAO, eat smart." **151** Two varieties of organic rice from the OAO collection. **152/5** A selection from the first two groups of products designed by Starck for the 7-11 convenience store chain in Japan, for personal hygiene goods and office products. Basic items, simply packaged and honestly presented, on a system designed to fit 7-11 standard shelving: cookware will be next. If Starck's work in 1998 has been dominated by the new disciplines of designing food packaging and "nonproducts for nonconsumers" with Good Goods and 7-11, he has also launched new furniture designs, showing his ongoing interest in both the technology and applications of furniture. **157/9** The Miss C.O.C.O folding chair designed by Starck for Cassina is an elegant exploration of the mechanical dynamics of a folding chair: an echo, in fact, of some of Starck's earliest furniture designs. **160/3** The Lazy Work Sofa designed by Starck for Cassina moves from minimal products to a reinvention of bourgeois elegance, via a sofa for the homeworking, sharing, twenty-first-century family. **164/5** The M.T. table designed by Starck for Cassina recalls the ONF table in its use of a central wooden beam as a support: this is an "exercise de style" in the art of furniture design. **166/7** Neoz chairs and tables designed by Starck for Driade, all about enabling sharing: a table the height of a bar allows some diners to stand, but the real chairs—rather than bar stools—mean that others can sit and share a meal in comfort.

ST GEORGES

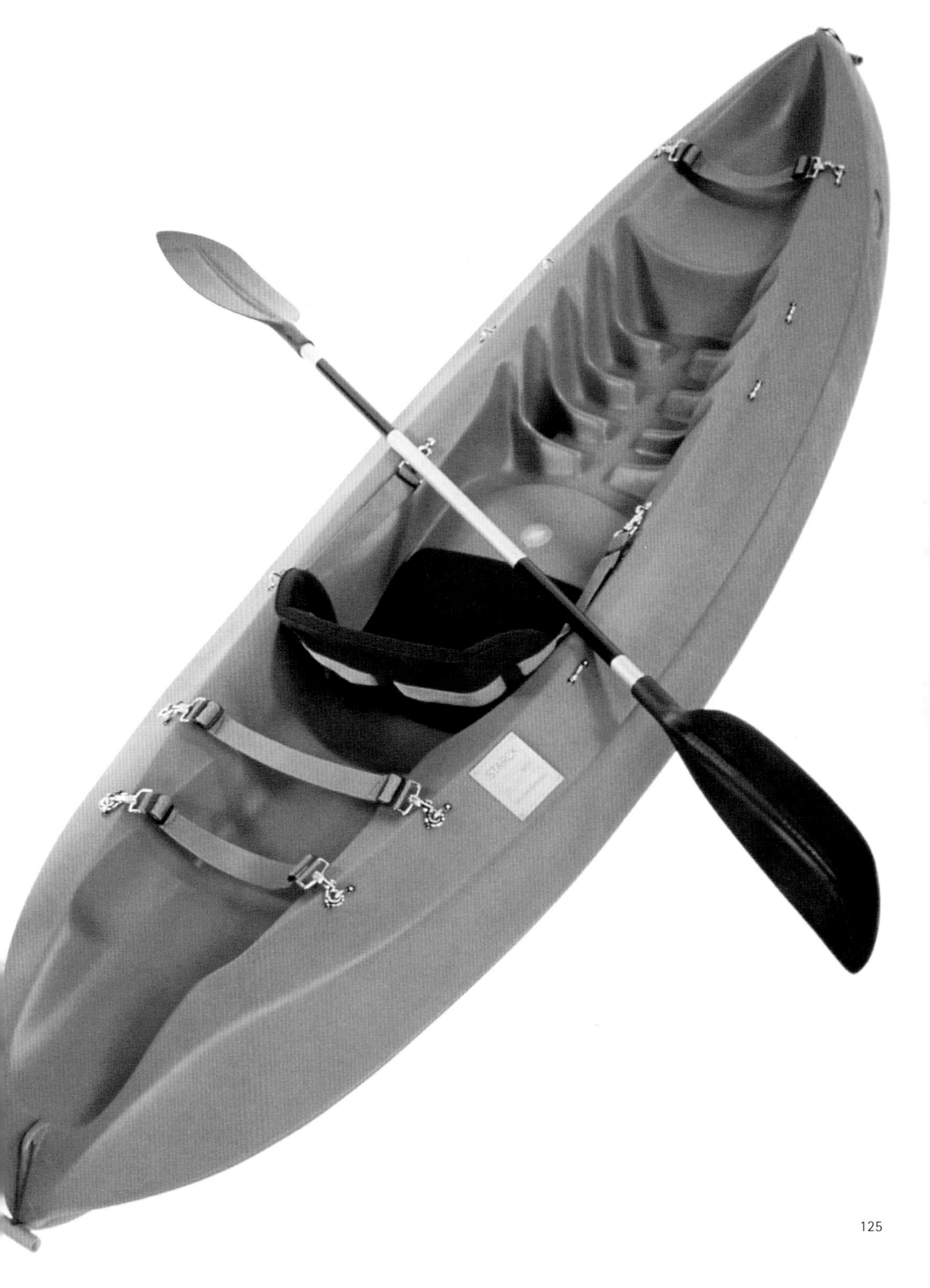

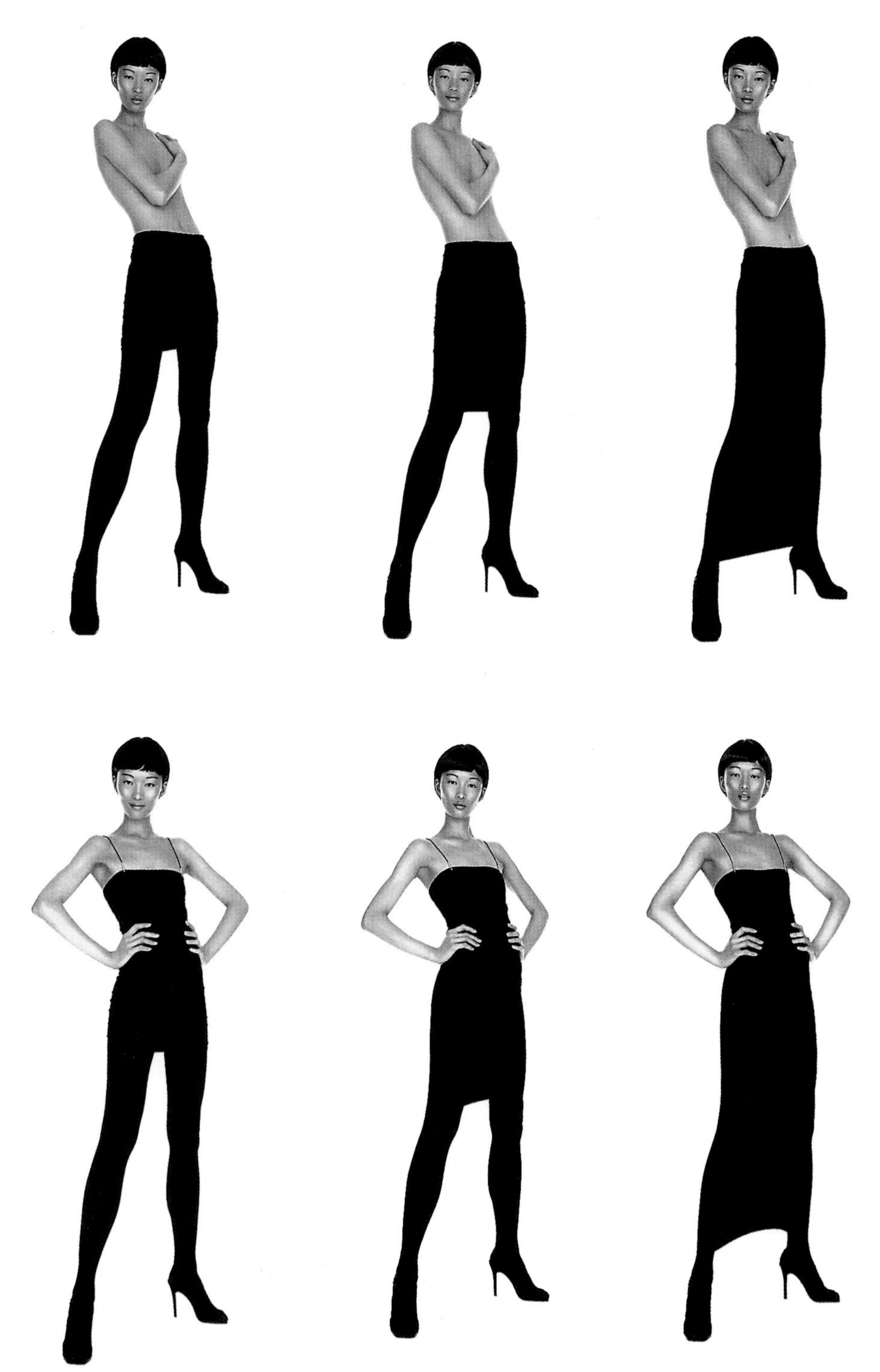

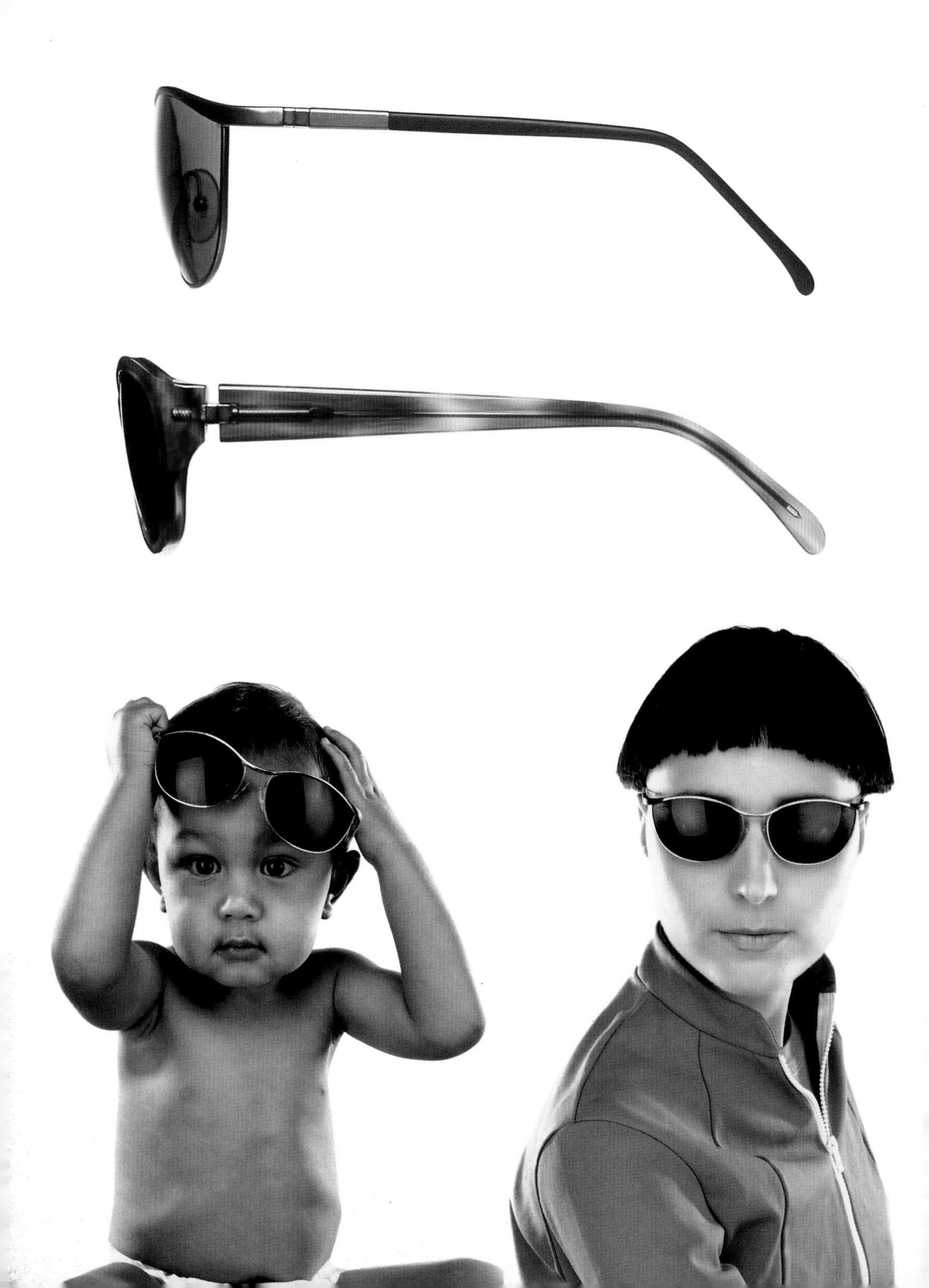

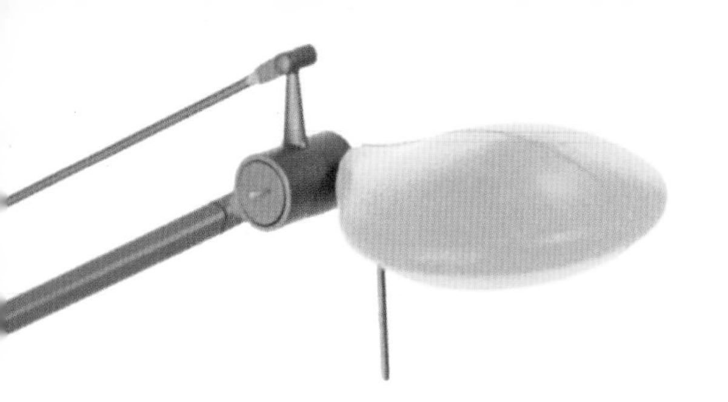

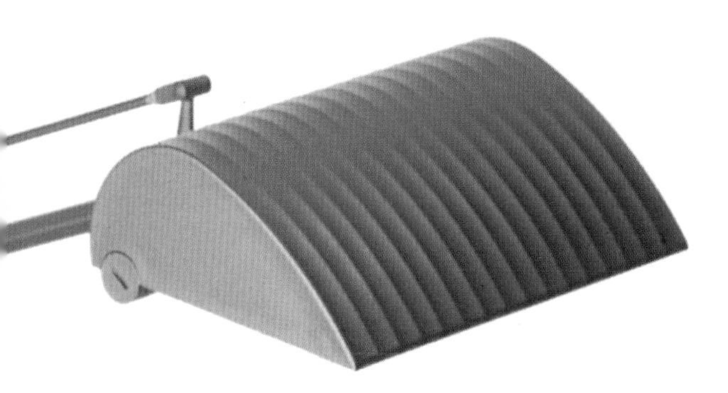

STARCK
with
Virgin
CONSCIENCE
CONSCIENCE
いしき

STARCK
with
Virgin
CORPS
BODY
からだ

STARCK
with
Virgin
COEUR
HEART
こころ

STARCK
WITH
Virgin
TÊTE
HEAD
りせい

Amin Zaoui

Je raconte à Hélène

COMME ÇA, par le hasard des hasards, nous nous sommes trouvés, côte à côte, œil dans l'œil, Hélène et moi.

Nous nous regardons. Nous grandissons un peu plus cet hiver, un peu plus encore l'été prochain.

Hélène aime le ciel. Elle rêve d'avoir un cheval ailé, Bourak, pour pouvoir monter jusqu'au bleu, là-bas, en haut, plus haut encore où Dieu, lumière sur lumière, sagesse absolue, avec sa barbe blanche, est assis pour l'éternité de l'éternité, sur un immense baldaquin impérial.

Hélène, par ses yeux remplis de ciel, m'aime, peut-être un peu moins que le ciel majestueux qu'elle veut toucher des doigts.

Ma voix n'est pas faite pour chanter, mais Hélène, qui aime la musique et imite avec excellence onze chants d'oiseaux, peut-être un peu plus, me demande souvent de lui chanter une chanson franco-arabe : « Chéri je t'aime, chéri je t'adore, Mostépha ya Mostépha ana ba hibbak ya Mostépha. »

Je n'aime pas ma voix. Hélène me disait : « Dans ta voix, il y a du sucre et une grande rivière de miel... » Je lance des éclats de rire. Je suis timide. Je la serre contre moi, hirondelle, et je compte jusqu'à cent soixante-trois, comme ça « un, deux, trois, soixante dix-sept... ». Je ne sais pas pourquoi je compte jusqu'à cent soixante-trois et non pas jusqu'à quatre-vingt-dix-neuf ou quarante ou cent dix ou n'importe quel nombre. À ce instants, Hélène, la tête posée sur ma poitrine, les nattes longues atteignant les fesses, compte à son tour mes respirations, en écoutant la parole capitale du cœur.

Quand je chante, Hélène me dit : « J'ai envie de pisser », quelque chose lui pince son petit cœur, quelque chose comme la peur ou le crépuscule.

Les yeux d'une chatte sauvage comblée de cieux et de néant me parlent sans rien dire.

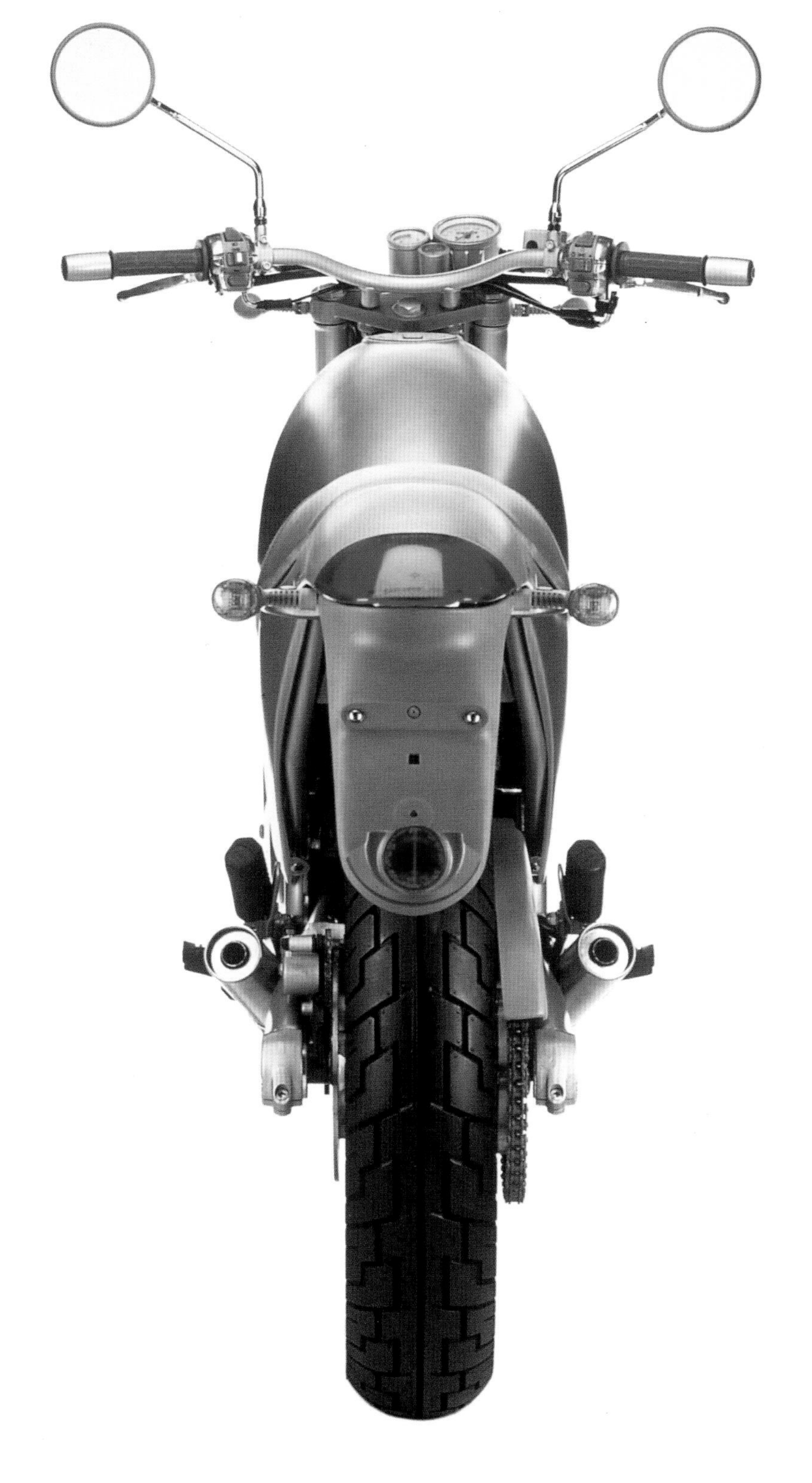

STARCK

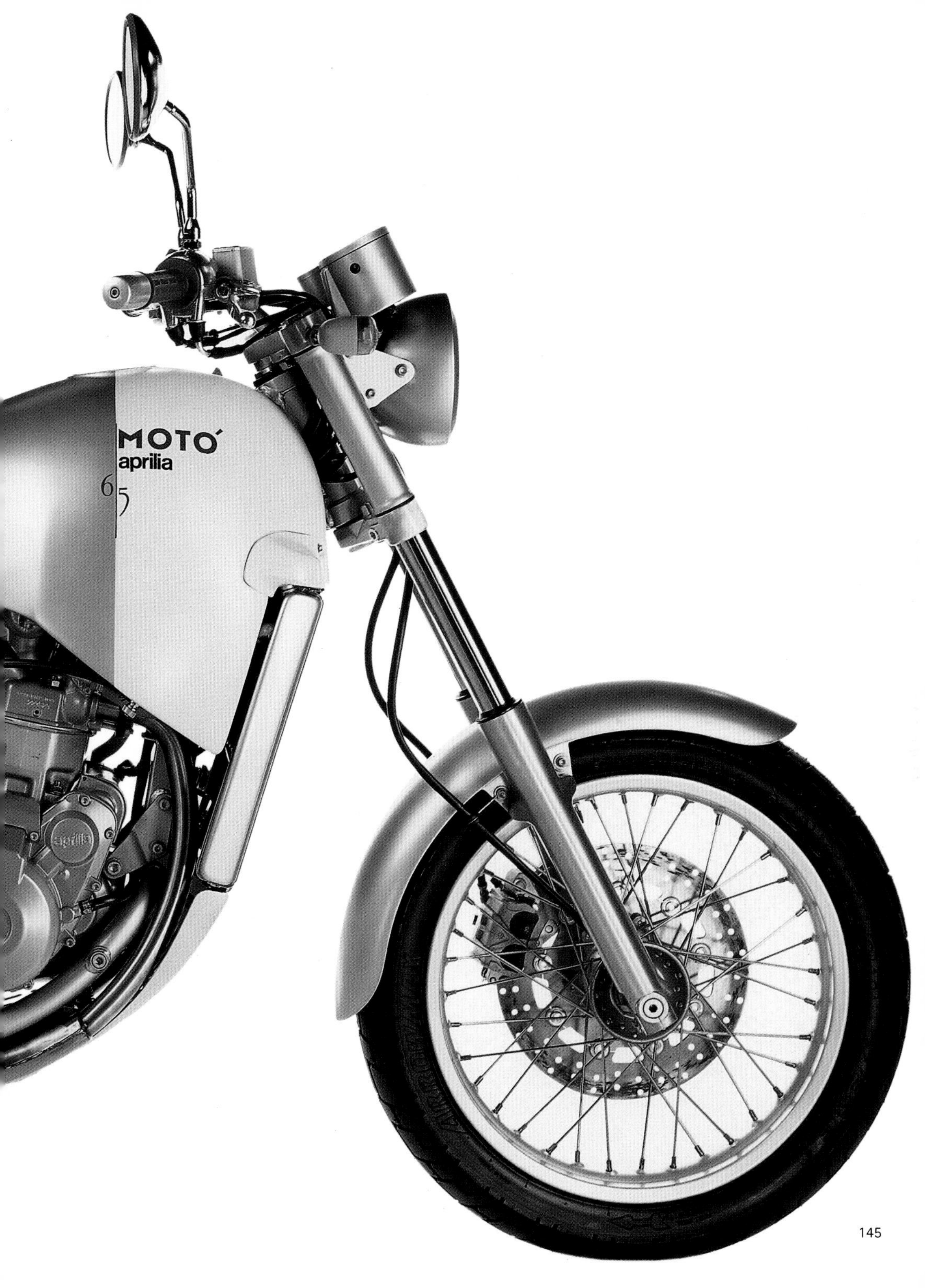
MOTÓ
aprilia
6
5

UN DÉTERGENT BON POUR L'HOMME: Les tablettes pour lave-vaisselle ECOVER sont sans phosphates et sans chlore. Outre les effets néfastes des phosphates sur l'environnement, leur production est très polluante : elle libère des métaux lourds et légèrement radioactifs contenant du gypse, inutilisable, qui doit être éliminé. Les détergents dérivés du sucre utilisés ici ont de très bonnes propriétés écologiques et sont doux pour la peau. **UN DÉTERGENT COMPÉTENT:** La préoccupation écologique est mise au même rang que le souci d'efficacité des produits. Les combinaisons chimiques étant moins stables et moins spectaculaires, la nature peut donc en venir à bout plus rapidement. La lessive n'en est pas moins efficace. L'utilisation de savon comme détersif à part entière, en combinaison avec des détergents d'origine végétale, garantit une très bonne action nettoyante. Produits lavants doux, ils n'attaqu nt pas les couleurs. L'absence de blanchissants et d'azurants optiques garantit la parfaite stabilité des couleurs. **UN DÉTERGENT MEILLEUR POUR LA NATURE:** Au lieu des composants pétrochimiques classiquement utilisés dans les produits nettoyants. ECOVER emploie essentiellement des matières premières organiques renouvelables et se décomposant rapidement dans le milieu naturel en eléments innofensifs. La réduction de la tension superficielle de l'eau provoquée par les tensio-actif (agents détergents) est fatale à la faune et a la flore aquatique. Elle est comparable pour l'homme à un changement de pression atmosphérique si violent que nous nous retrouverions collés au plafond sous la forme d'une petite tâche de couleur rouge. ECOVER restaure la tension artificielle. **MODE D'EMPLOI:** Retirer les restes de nourriture de la vaisselle. Contrôler la propreté du filtre et ajouter, si

STARCK®

WITH

ECOVER®

TABLETTES POUR LAVE-VAISSELLE

UN ASSOUPLISSANT BON POUR L'HOMME :
d'allergies, il ne contient pas d'azurants optiques.
difficilement dégradables présents dans les
produisent l'effet " plus blanc que blanc ", effet
puisqu'ils ne sont ni lavants, ni hygiéniques,
les rayons UV et de masquer ainsi les tâches
En revanche, ils sont à la base de
nées graves, allergies,
dans la guérison des plaies,
contact quasi-permanent avec des
portant des traces de produits
assouplissant contient un
végétale plus sain pour la peau.
COMPÉTENT : la préoccupation
mise au même rang que le
produits. Les combinaisons
moins stables et moins
peut en venir à bout plus
cissant n'en est pas moins efficace.
est inférieure à celle des
en revanche l'absorption d'humidité, freinée en
de l'adoucissant et du textile, est meilleure.
MEILLEUR POUR LA NATURE : au lieu des composants
classiques, ECOVER emploie essentiellement
premières organiques renouvelables et se décomposant
dans le milieu naturel en éléments innofensifs.
superficielle de l'eau provoquée par les
détergents) est fatale à la faune et à la flore aquatique.
pour l'homme à un changement de pression
violent que nous nous retrouverions collés au
d'une petite tâche de couleur rouge. ECOVER
artificielle. STARCK with ECOVER : Philippe
d'utilisateur responsable, a choisi ECOVER pour la
gamme de produits ménagers efficaces, sans parfum,
possibles pour l'homme et l'environnement.
STARCK
ECOVER
ASSOUPLISSANT
CONCENTRÉ

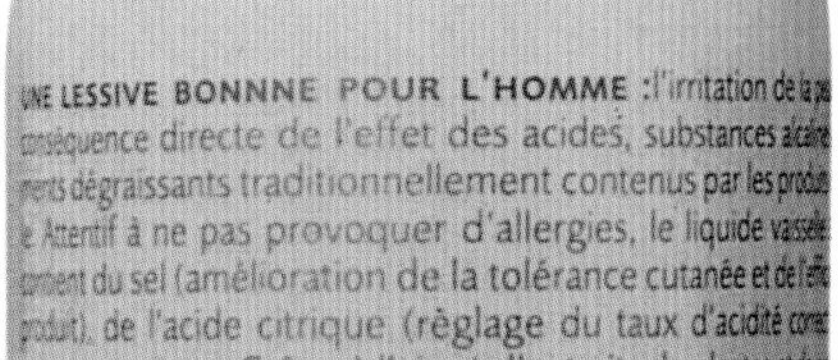

UNE LESSIVE BONNNE POUR L'HOMME :
conséquence directe de l'effet des acides, substances
dégraissants traditionnellement contenus par les
Attentif à ne pas provoquer d'allergies, le liquide
du sel (amélioration de la tolérance cutanée et de
de l'acide citrique (règlage du taux d'acidité
Grâce à l'ajout d'extraits de plantes et de
est très doux pour les mains.
COMPÉTENTE : la préoccupation
mise au même rang que le souci d'efficacité
duits. Les combinaisons chimiques
stables et moins spectaculaires,
venir à bout plus rapidement. Très
dégraissage et le nettoyage de la
de son caractère concentré en
doser que la moitié de la quantité
de vaisselle. La quantité de
importante que dans un liquide classique.
gent non-ionique à base de sucre,
détergent anionique et amphotère
bon dégraissage et une formation de mousse stable.
MEILLEURE POUR LA NATURE : au lieu de
classiques, ECOVER emploie essentiellement des
organiques renouvelables et se décomposant
milieu naturel en éléments innofensifs. La
de l'eau provoquée par les
détergents) est fatale à la faune et à la flore aquatique.
pour l'homme à un changement de pression
que nous nous retrouverions collés au plafond
tâche de couleur rouge. ECOVER restaure la
responsabilité ne doit pas s'arrêter au
DOSAGE : consommation minimale : 1 jet (± 2ml)
Ce produit nettoie parfaitement sans mousser
vos responsabilités écologiques. CE PRODUIT
TENT : un dosage correct garantit un résultat optimal et un
STARCK
WITH
ECOVER
LESSIVE LIQUIDE
CONCENTRÉE

OLIO EXTRA VERGINE
DI OLIVA BIOLOGICA
SAN VITO

OLIO EXTRA VERGINE
DI OLIVA BIOLOGICA
Nous sommes
mangeons.
écosystème
indissociable
nourriture.
créatif à une

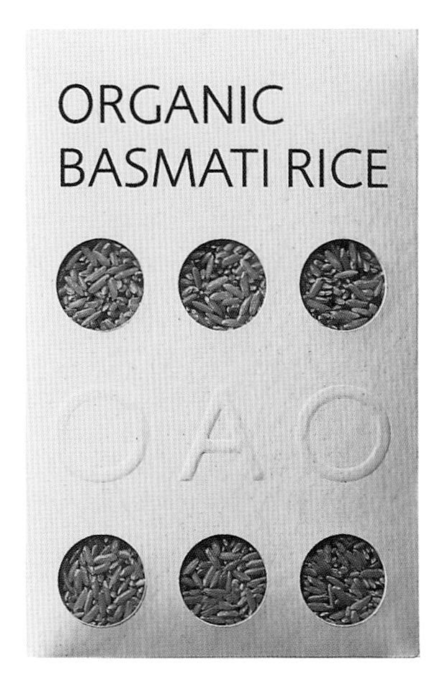
ORGANIC
BASMATI RICE
OAO

ORGANIC
THAI RICE
OAO

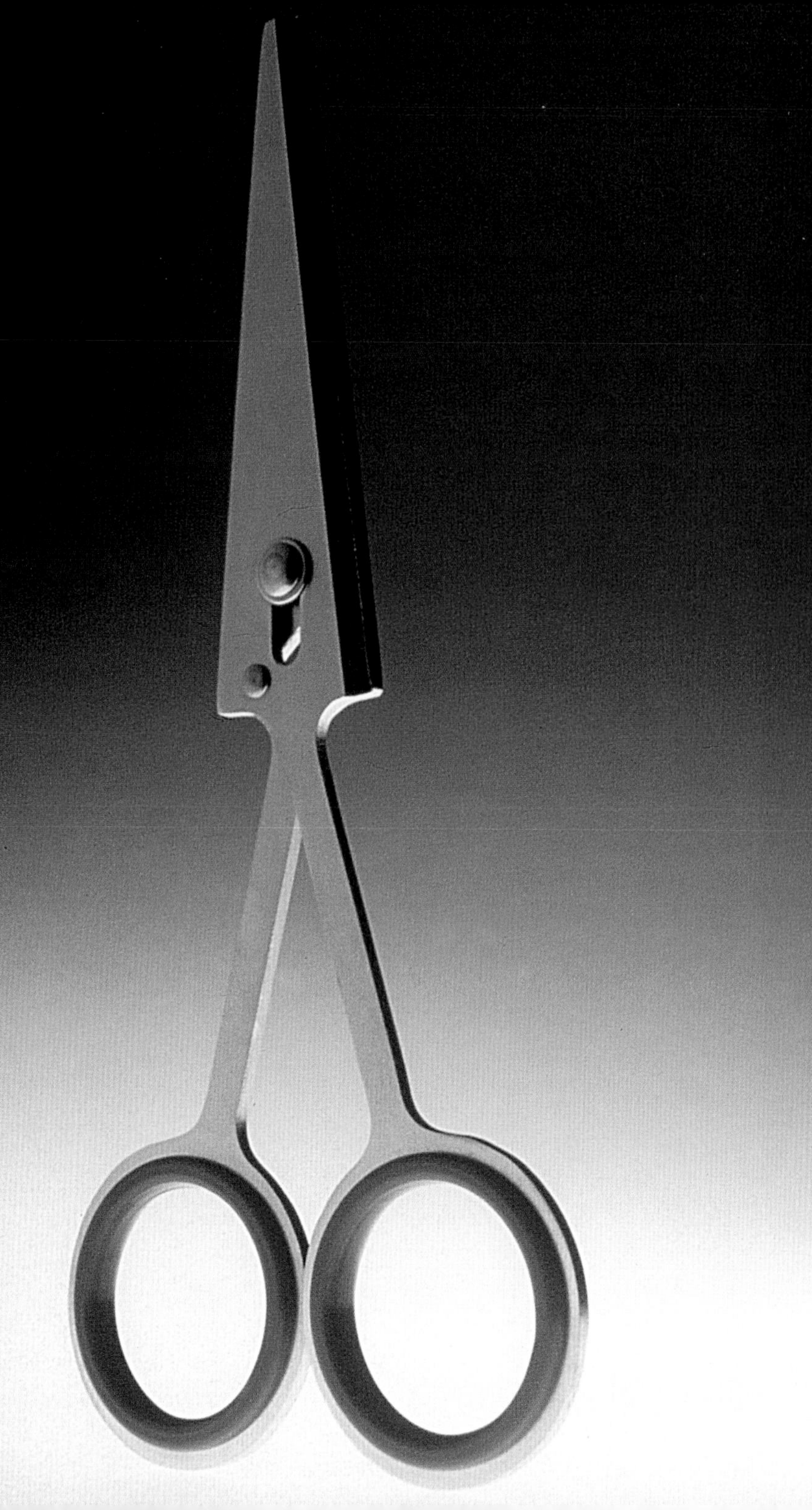

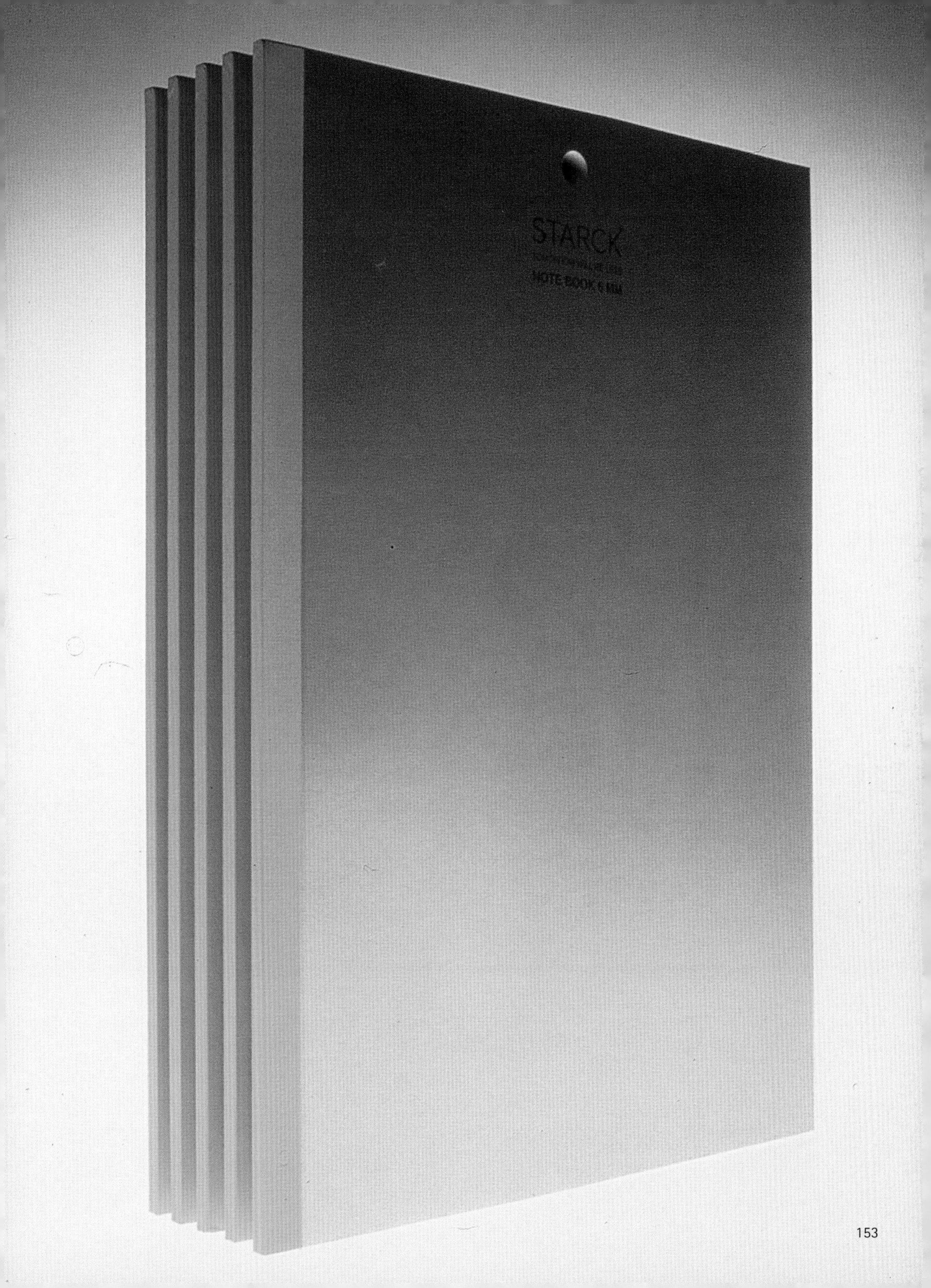
STARCK

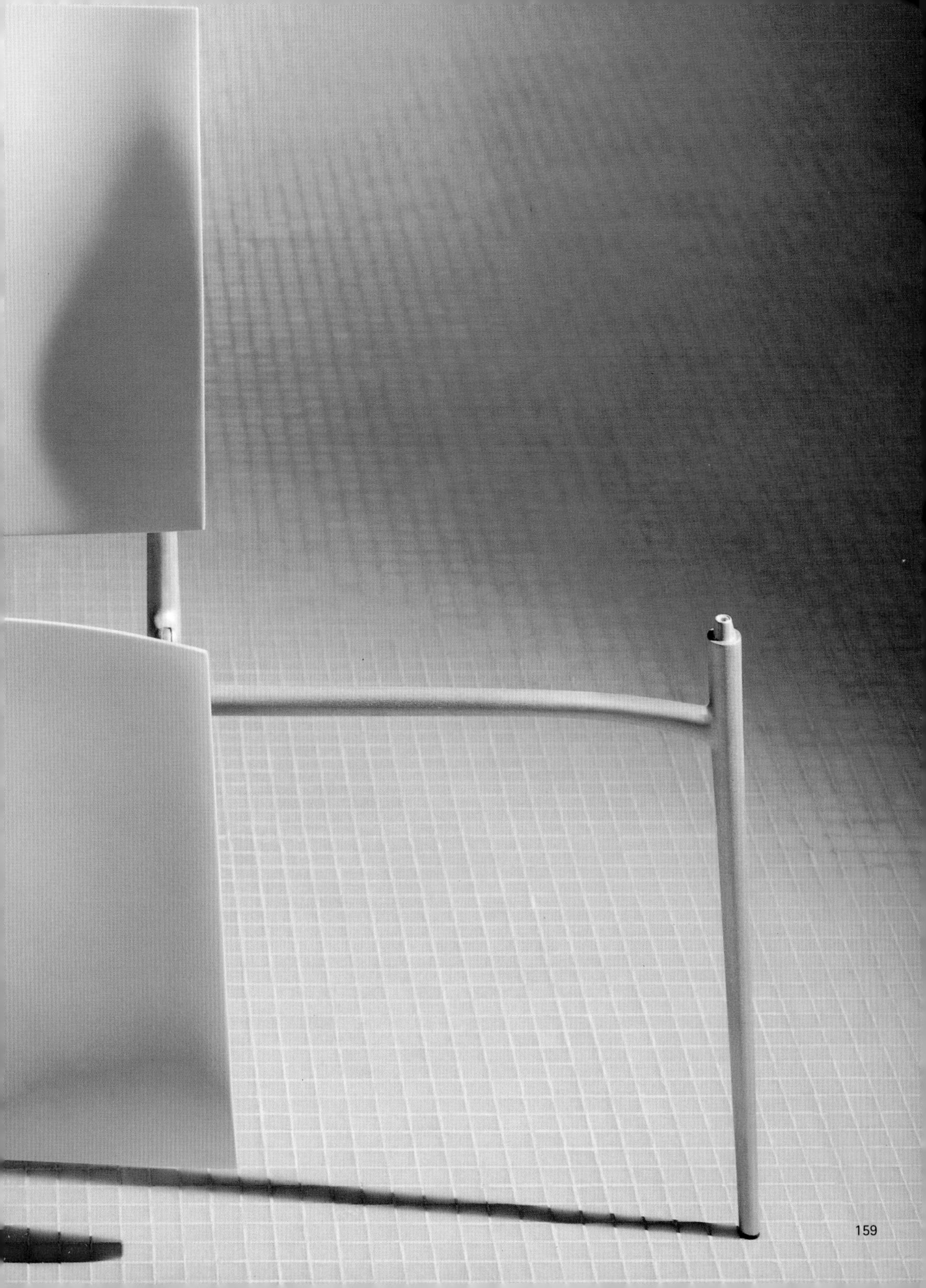

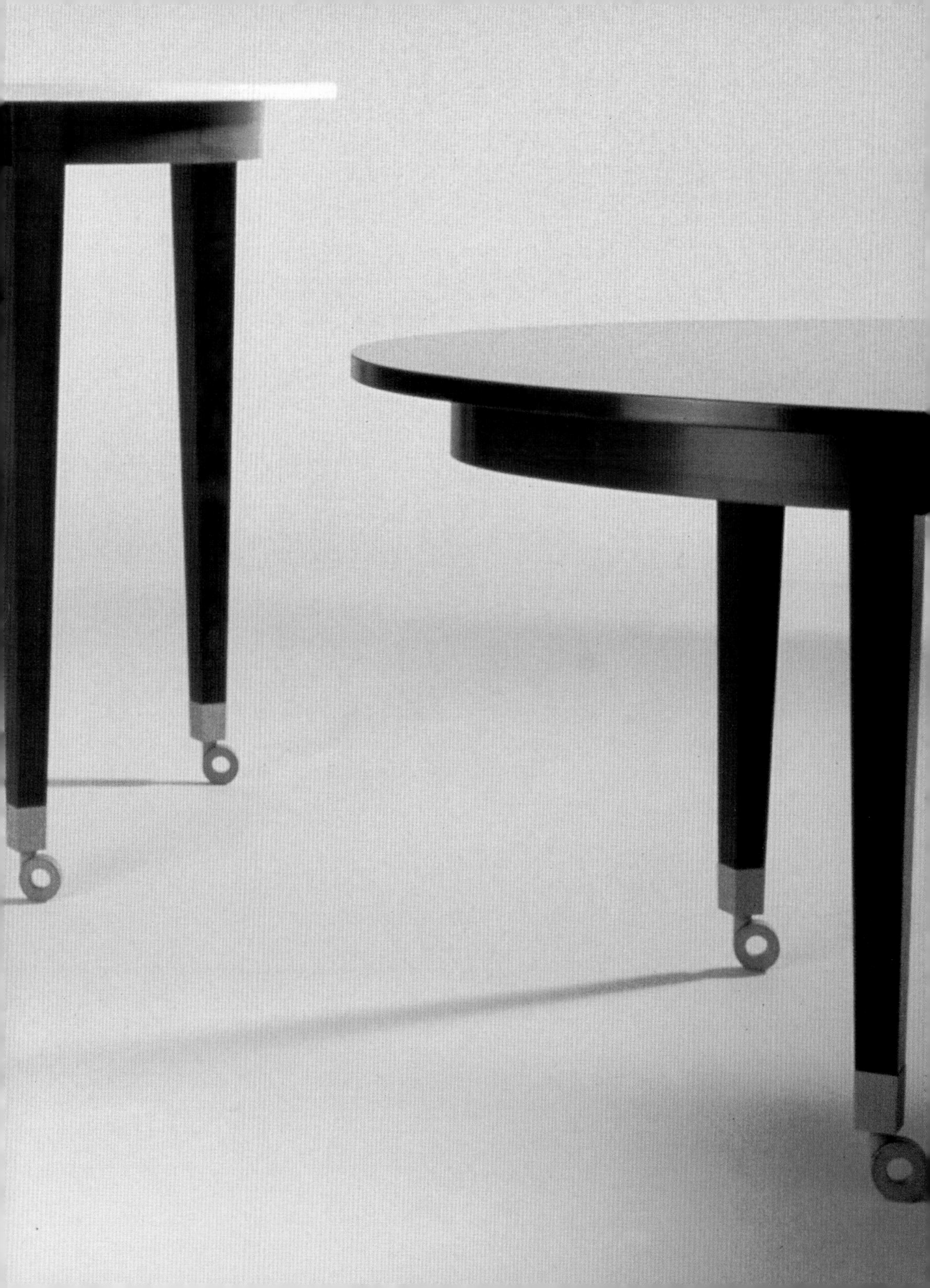

Welcome

If there is a broad theme that runs through Starck's interior design practice, from the earliest work at La Main Bleue in 1976 to his current hotel projects with Ian Schrager, it is the sheer pleasure he takes in making people welcome, whether as guests in hotels, bars, and restaurants, or as shoppers or office workers. Over the next thirty pages we explore this world of hospitality. **170/1** Café Costes, Paris, 1984. Once the coolest spot in Les Halles, Paris, now closed, but Starck is designing the restaurant for the nearby Pompidou Center's reopening in the year 2000. **172/3** View of Tokyo business district from under the tail surmounting the Asahi building, 1990: a firm of submarine engineers was called in to construct it, but whether it is a fish or a flame is left to the imagination. **174** Interior staircase at the Asahi Beer Hall. **175** Godzilla lives! The humped roof of the Nani Nani office building in Tokyo, 1989. **176** The Baron Vert office building in Osaka, 1990, seen from the Buddhist cemetery behind it. **177** The original drawings suggested a red building: but the more natural green color makes the building even stranger. **178/9** The entrance lobby and a room door at the Royalton Hotel, New York, Starck's first project with Ian Schrager, in 1988. **180/1** Room details at the Royalton Hotel. **182/3** Door and wall detailing at the Paramount Hotel, New York, 1990. **184/5** Room settings and the main entrance at the Delano in Miami, 1995, a deliberately cool, contrasting space. **186/9** The Felix Restaurant and Oyster Bar in the Peninsula Hotel, Hong Kong, 1994: the tribe awaits. **190/1** The lobby and restaurant-bar at the Mondrian Hotel in Los Angeles, 1997: soft, unreal colors for Tinseltown. The success lies in the combination of elements, not all designed by Starck, and attention to detail. **192/3** The pool at the Mondrian Hotel, Los Angeles. **194** Exteriors at the Mondrian Hotel, including the outdoor restaurant created with giant flowerpots. The hotels opened to date with Schrager have a common sense of style and elegance, but with an individual character in each case. **196/7** The entrance stair at the Restaurant Theatron, Mexico City, 1985. **198** The entrance to the Manin Restaurant, Tokyo, 1987. **199** The staircase at the Salon Coppola in Milan, 1992. These last three items show how the use of theatrical gesture becomes more muted and supple in the development of Starck's work, while the importance of certain elements, such as staircase detailing, remains critical.

3'-0"

At Home

Unlike other furniture and product designers who have worked for both business and domestic markets, the main focus of Starck's design has been for the individual and for the home. This is not fortuitous, but the result of a longstanding policy of making the individual the political as well as the design beneficiary of his work. The closing pages of this book recall some of his work in this context. **202/3** The Trois Suisses house. **204** Concept drawing for the Le Moult house, Issy-les-Moulineaux. **205** Exterior of the Le Moult House. **206** Dr. No chairs, 1996, and Miss Trap tables, 1997, both by Kartell. **207** Stacked Dr. No chairs. **208** Miss Trip chair, 1996, by Kartell, showing the pack-flat system and components. **209** Monsieur X and Monsieur X Rocking, folding chairs for XO, 1996. **210** Bubu stools, first produced in 1991 with a second color range in 1996, for XO. **211** Prince Aha stools, by Kartell, 1996. **212** The 1985 Ara stool for VIA: the designs on the side are by Starck's daughter, Ara, then aged four. **213** The Dadada stool, 1993. **214** The WW stool, 1990, for Vitra, based on the proposal for an office for Wim Wenders. **215** Olly Tango stacking chair, 1994. **216/7** Stacked and and single Louis XX chairs for Vitra, 1992. **218/9** Stacked and single Lord Yo chairs for Fedra, 1993. **220/1** Detail from a photo portrait of Starck by Jean-Baptiste Mondino: the idea came to Mondino when Starck came into his studio, and he drew the images on the sitter's chest from memory. **222** Miss Sissi lamp for Flos, 1990. **223** Starck with the Romeo Moon lamp for Flos, 1995. **224** Oa lamp for Flos, 1996: Starck's son, Oa, was born in 1996. **225** Pour la vie, 1990, a marble vase with glass "flowers" for Alessi. **226** Tap for Hansgrohe, 1994. **227** Bathtub for Duravit, 1994. **228** Excalibur toilet brush for Heller, 1996. **229** Joe Cactus ashtray for Alessi, 1990. **230** Mister MeuMeu cheese grater for Alessi, 1992. **231** Max le Chinois colander for Alessi, 1991. **233** MoaMoa radio for Thomson, 1994 (top left), and three remote controls from the same collection. **234** Alo voice-operated telephone for Thomson (design Gérôme Olivet), 1996. **235** Perso video-conferencing tablet for Thomson (design Matali Crasset), 1996. **236/7** Zéo television for Thomson, 1994–95. **238** Rock'nRock mini hi-fi audio system for Thomson/Telefunken, 1996 (design Elsa Frances). **239** Starck as Ganesh in an image by Jean-Baptiste Mondino.

Starck House (3 Suisses) 1994

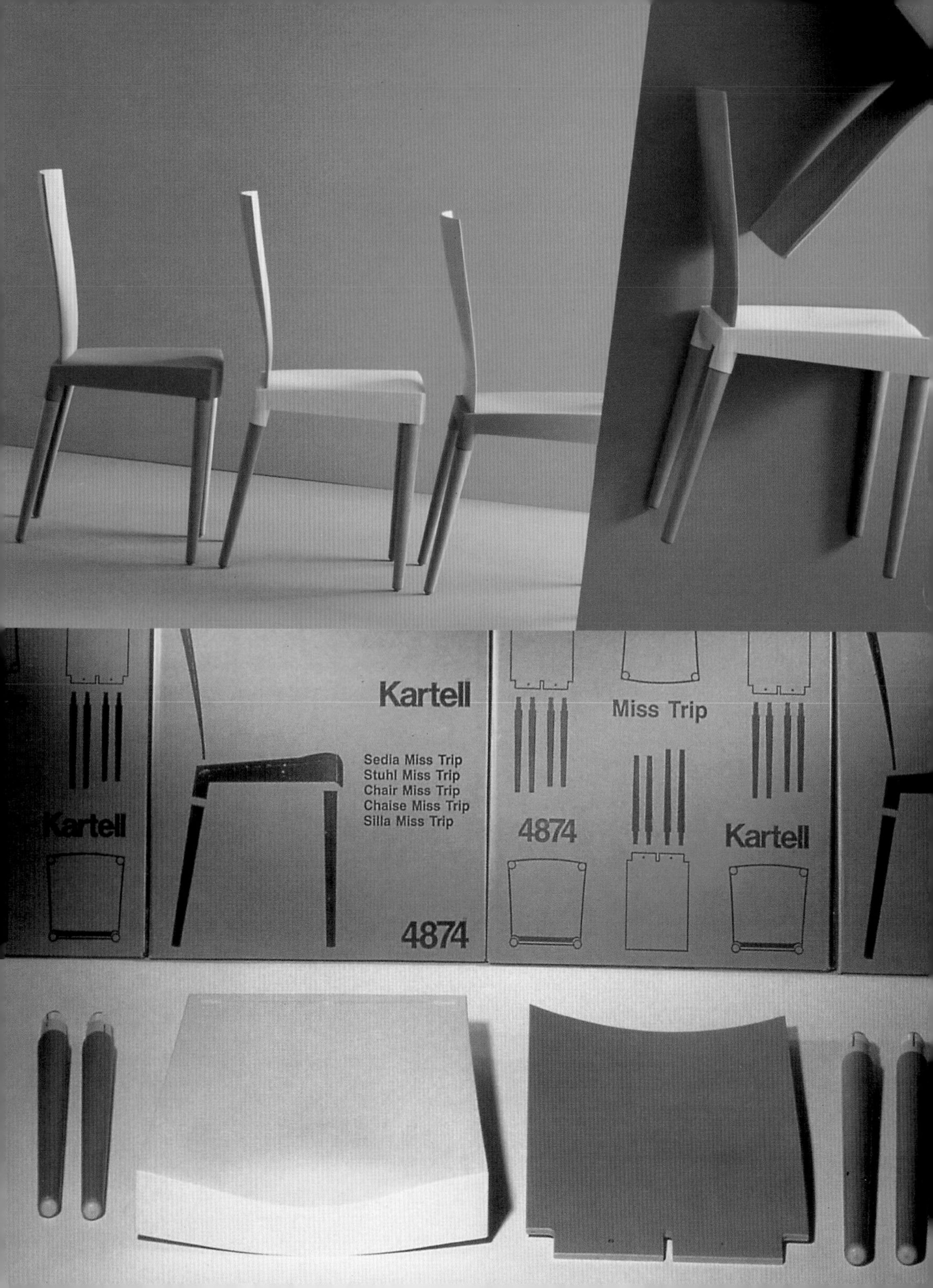
Kartell
Sedia Miss Trip
Stuhl Miss Trip
Chair Miss Trip
Chaise Miss Trip
Silla Miss Trip
4874
Miss Trip
4874
Kartell
Kartell

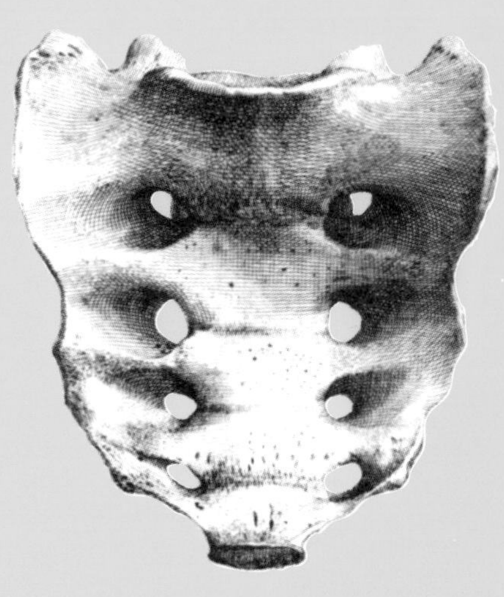

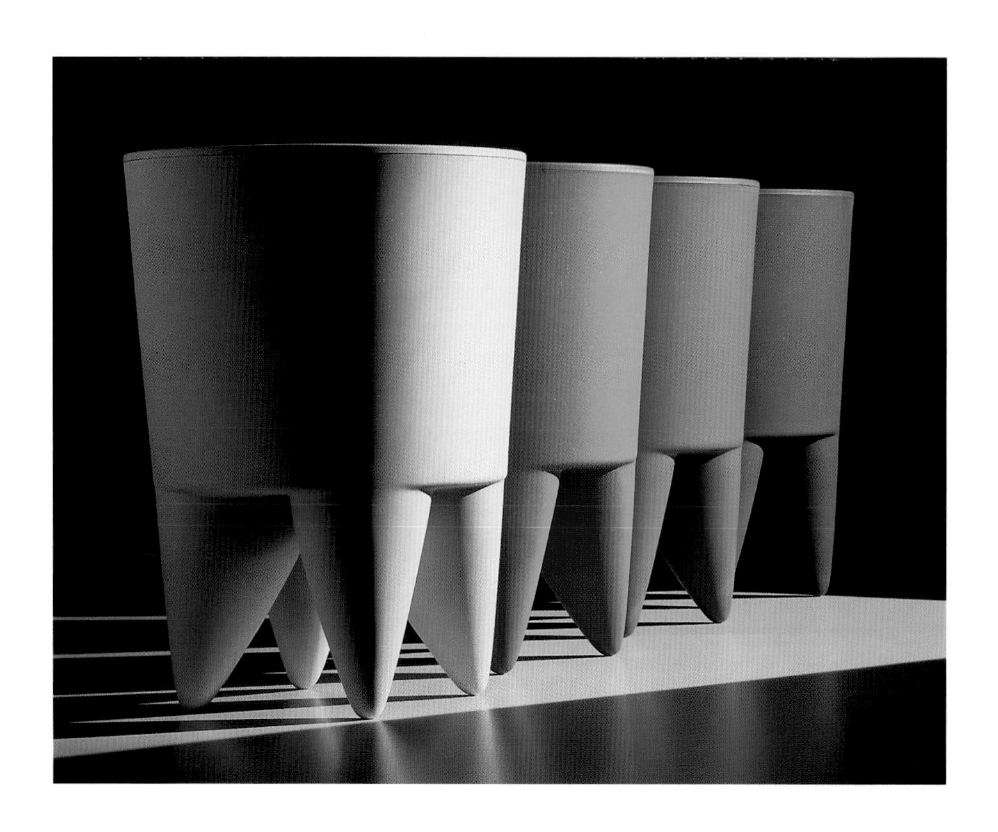

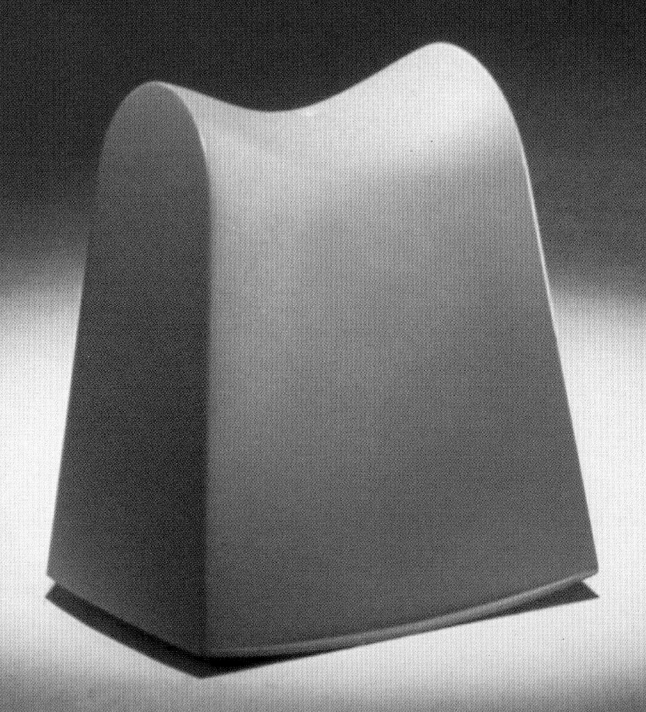

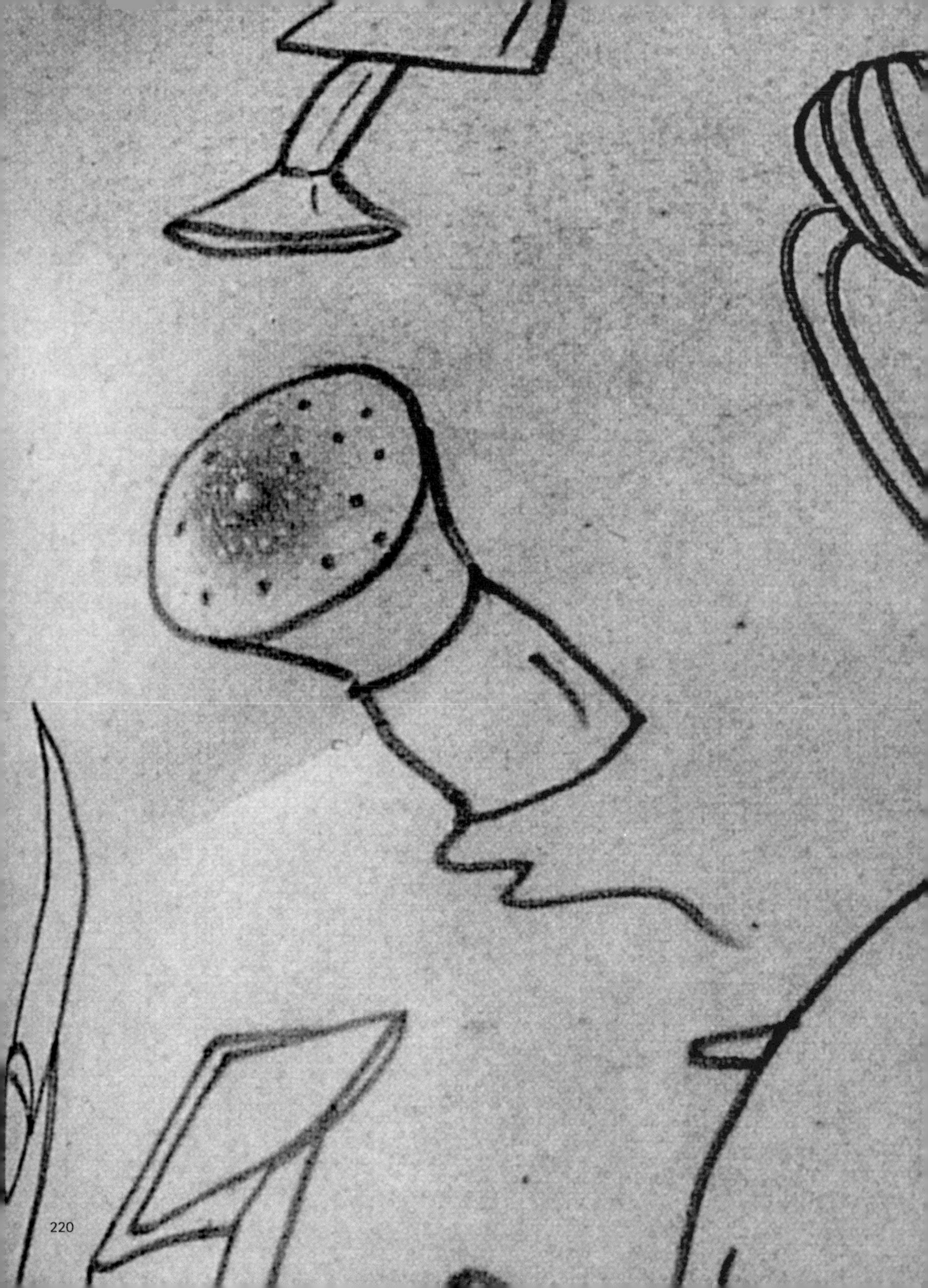

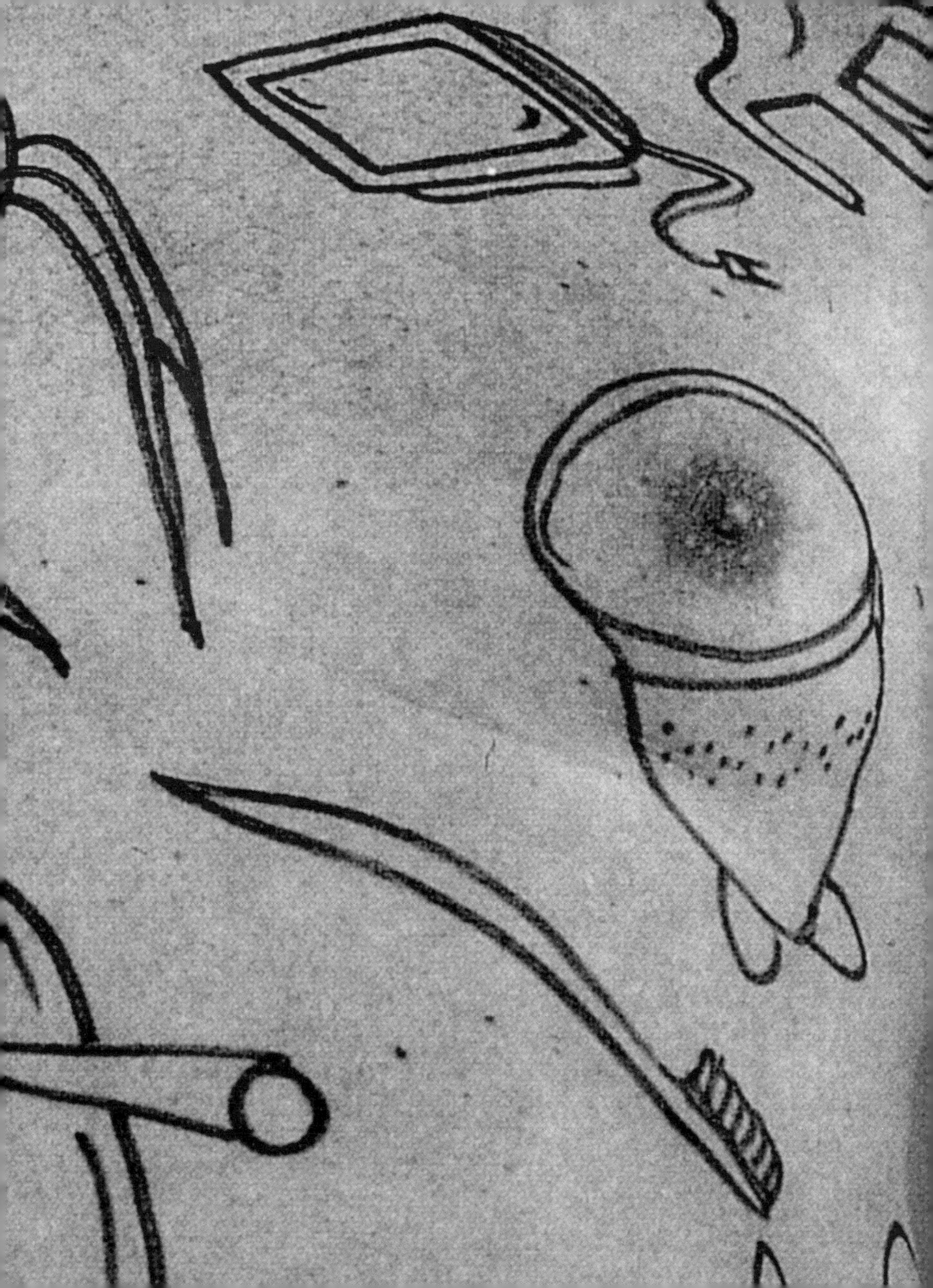

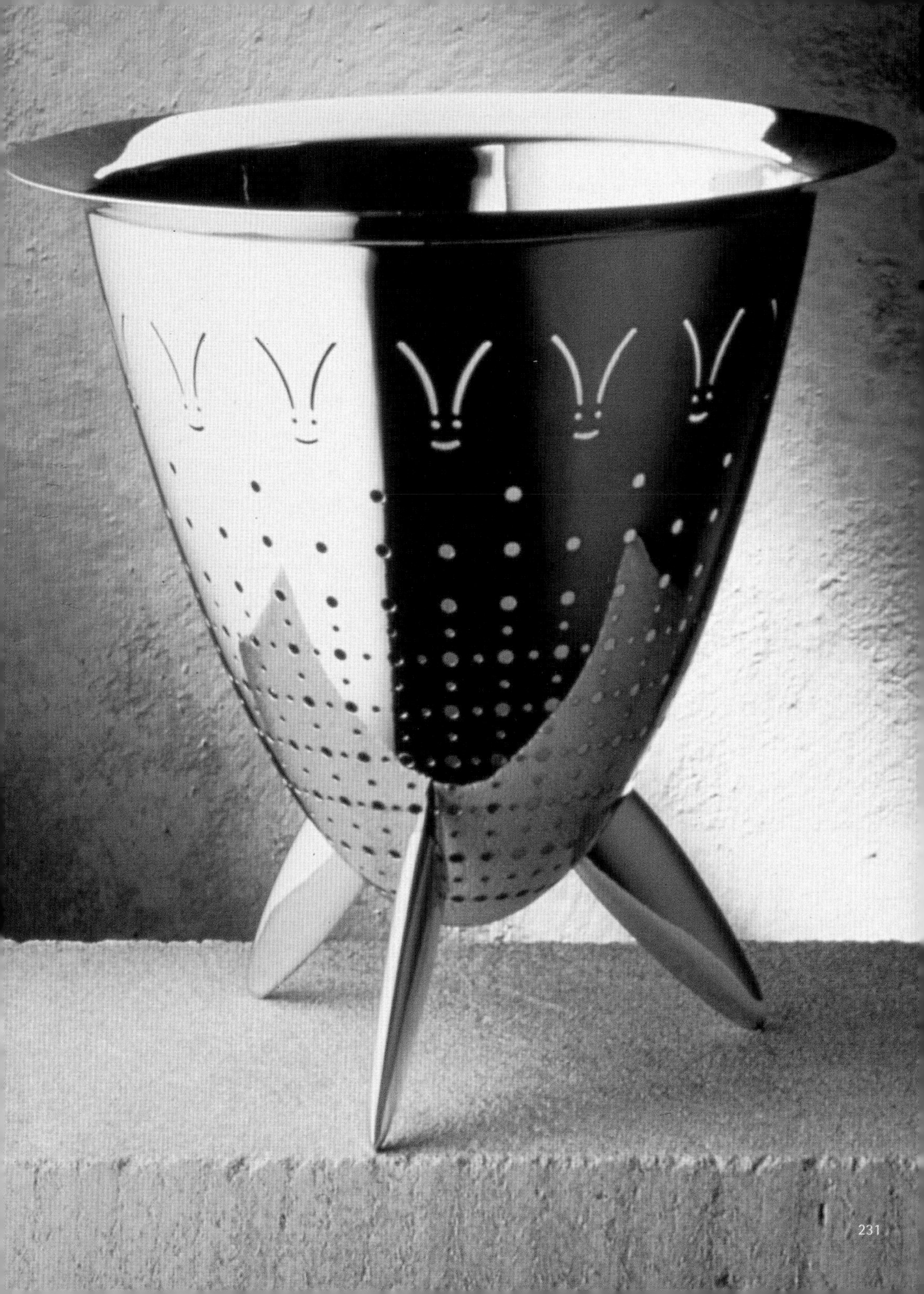

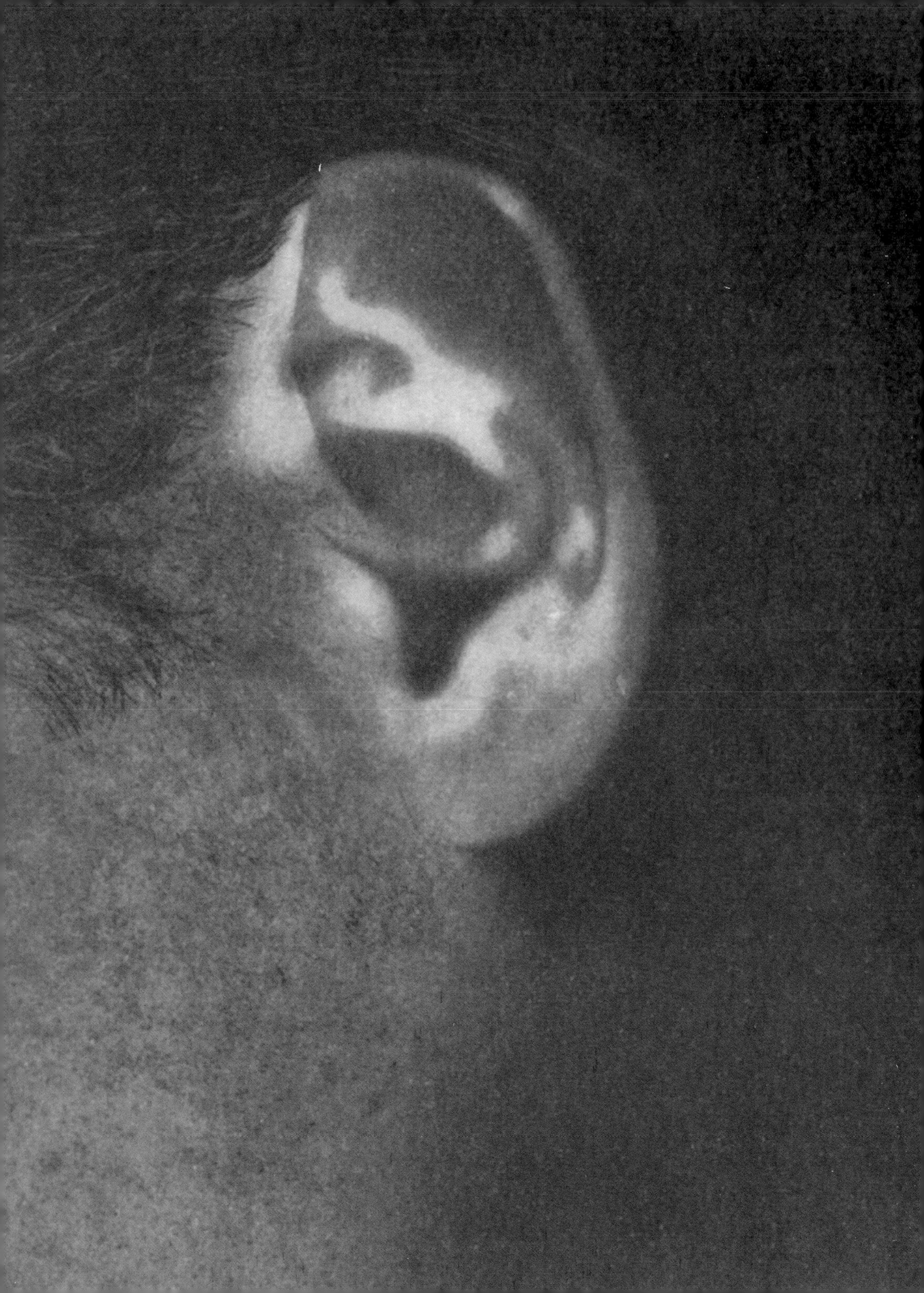

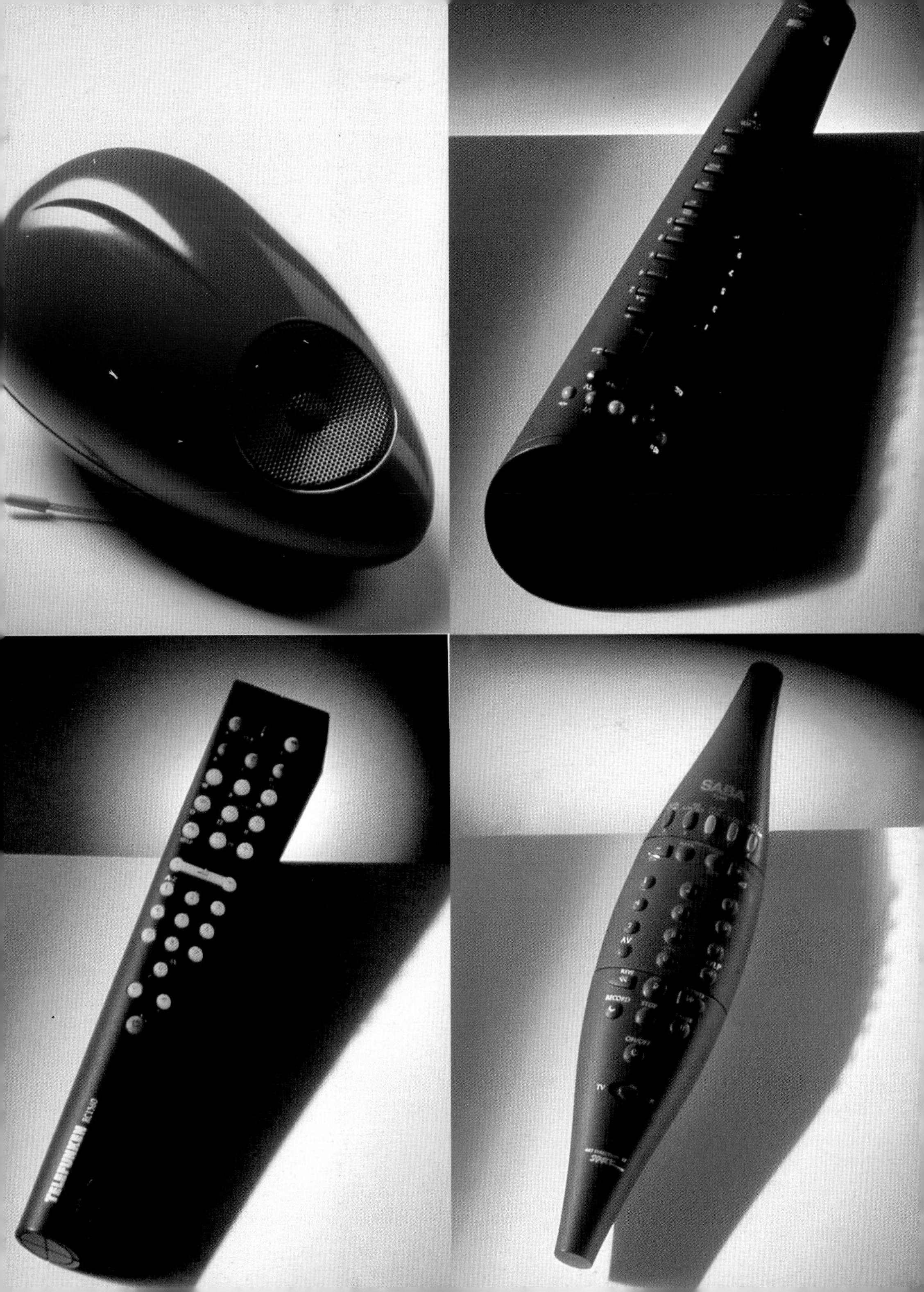
TELEFUNKEN
SABA
AV
REW
RECORD
STOP
ON/OFF
TV

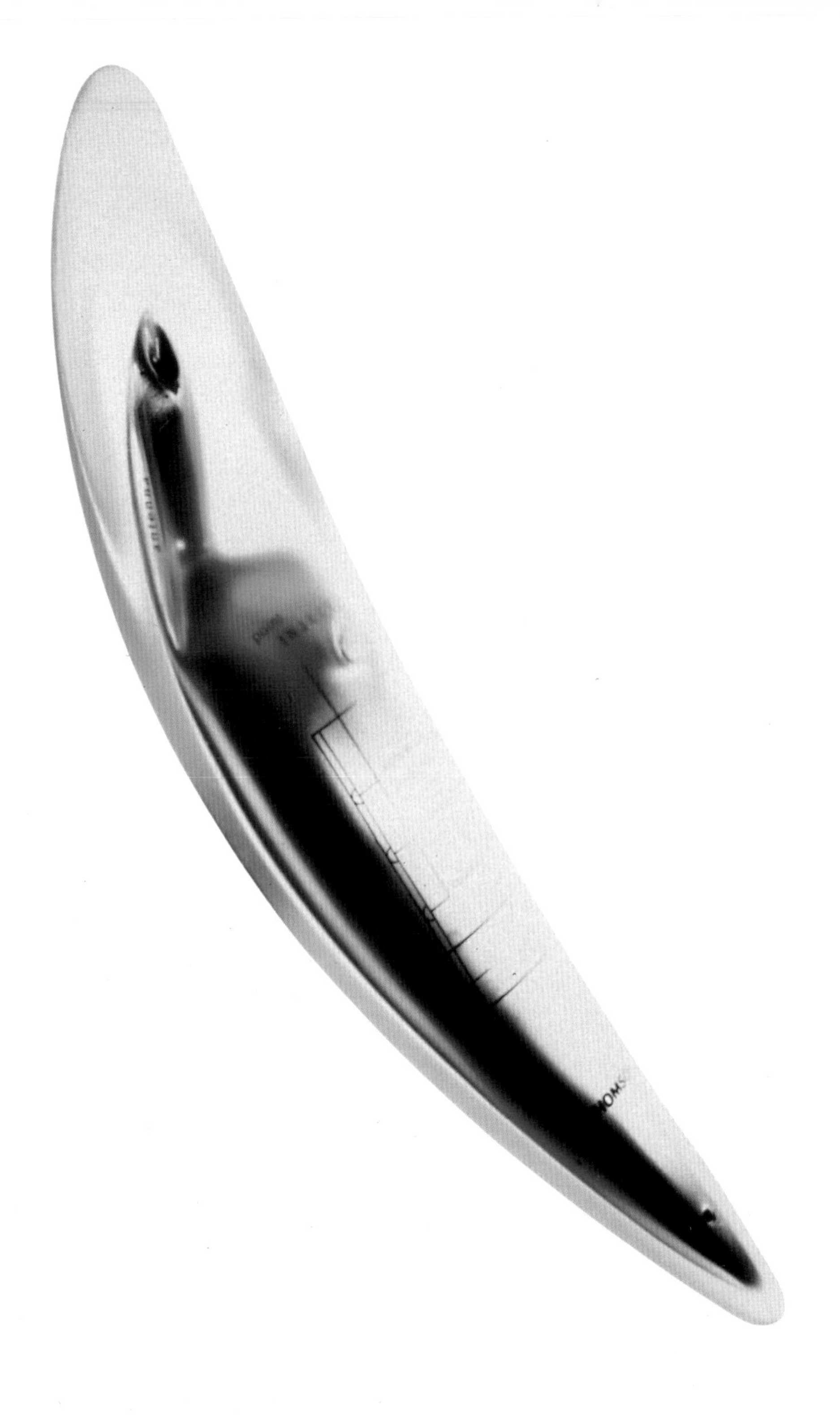

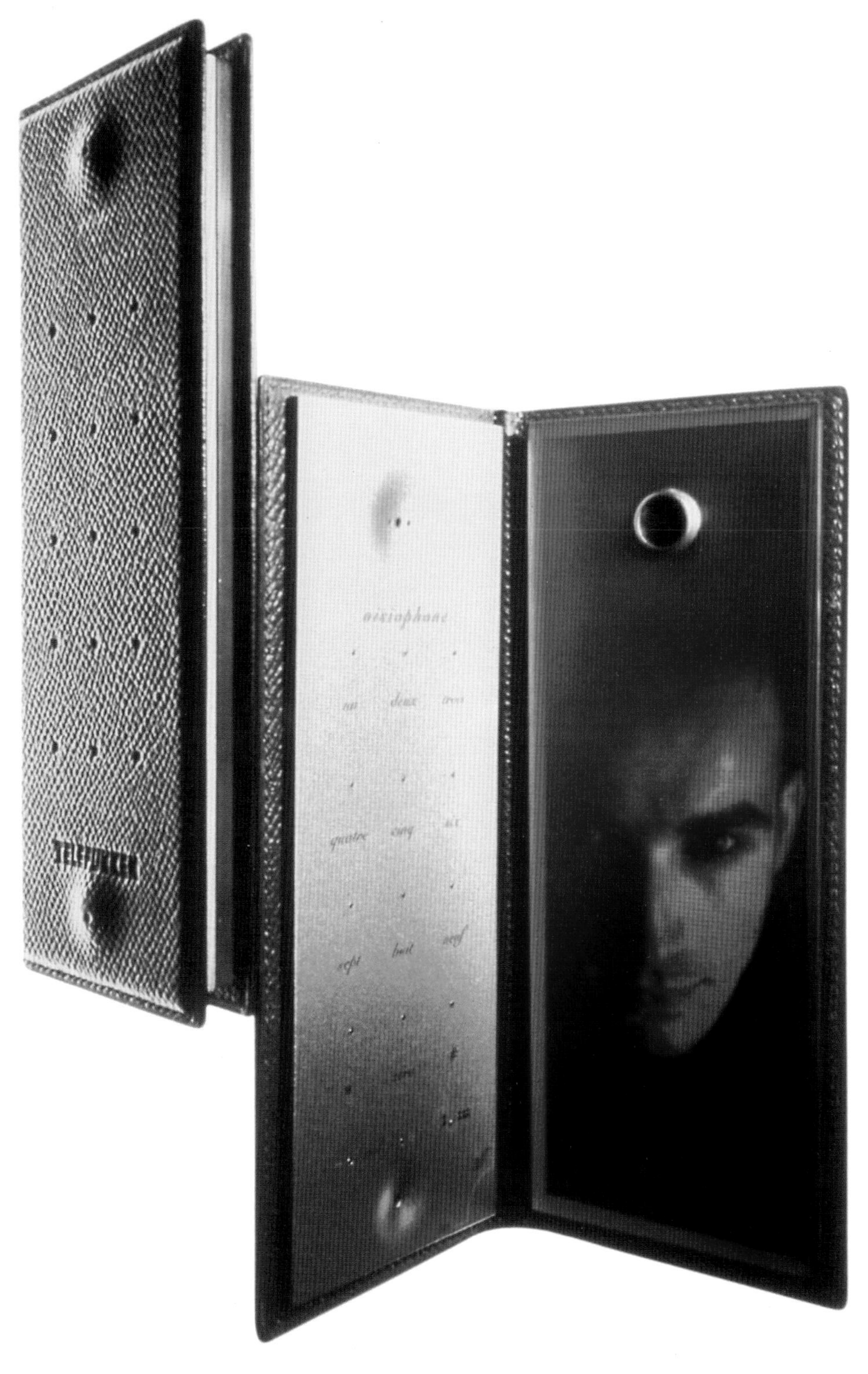
TELEFUNKEN
un deux trois
quatre cinq six
sept huit neuf

wireless
TELEFUNKEN rock

The author and publisher would like to thank the following photographers and companies for the illustrated material used in this book

Fabrizio Bergamo
Stéphane Couturier
Jacques Dirand
Michel Leliévre
Keith Lovegrove
Guido Mocafico
Jean-Baptiste Mondino
Jean Philippe Piter

Gianni Sabadin
Rudolf Schmutz
Andreas Sütterlin
Hervé Ternisien
Tom Vack
Alessi
Baleri
Benetau

Cassina
Driade
Duravit
Etcetera
Flos
Fluocaril
Hulton Getty
Kartell

La Redoute
Les Trois Suisses
OWO
Science Photo Library
Thomson
VIA
Vitra
XO